THE
POWER
OF LEGACY

THE PERSONAL HEROES OF AMERICA'S
MOST INSPIRING PEOPLE

THE
POWER
OF LEGACY

THE PERSONAL HEROES OF AMERICA'S MOST INSPIRING PEOPLE

BY RANDY SUTTON

LEGACY MEDIA

LEGACY MEDIA

LEGACY MEDIA
3325 Hastings Ave. Las Vegas Nevada 89107
www.thepoweroflegacy.com

For information on special discounts, bulk purchases, and sales promotions, email info@thepoweroflegacy.com

For excerpting permission, author information, or other inquiries, please contact the publisher at info@thepoweroflegacy.com

Cover design by Dale Sprague, Canyon Creative, Las Vegas
Interior design by Gwyn Kennedy Snider, GKS Creative, Nashville

First Printing 2014

Inspiration – Non-Fiction   2. Memoir – Non-Fiction
          3. Business – Non-Fiction   4. Biography – Non-Fiction

First Paperback Edition

ISBN 978-0-9906275-0-0

PRINTED IN THE UNITED STATES OF AMERICA

Dedication

It is to the memory of my parents Art and Lillian Sutton that I dedicate this book. Their love was a constant in my life. Unyielding, comforting and given without conditions. Not only did they give me life itself but a lifetime of inspiration as well.

Acknowledgments

Writing is often a solitary experience, but creating a book is a culmination of hard work, inspiration, encouragement and cooperation involving many people, especially in an anthology like *THE POWER OF LEGACY*. I am incredibly fortunate to have had so many people believe in this book and the effect that it could have on readers everywhere. I especially owe a debt of gratitude to the men and women who gave me not just their time for the interviews that made this book possible but giving of themselves while revealing their inspirations and often painful memories.

I am thankful to have had the advice and wise counsel of Antionette Kuritz and her team at Strategies Literary Public Relations in San Diego. She has been my friend for many years and the La Jolla Writers Conference which she founded has been a wonderful inspiration and source of "creative energy restoration" for not just me, but hundreds of other writers throughout the years.

True friends play a tremendous role in the lives of many writers, and I am one of them. My oldest and dearest friends, John and Pete Soderman, whom I consider more my brothers than my friends, were there for me at every step of my journey. If it had not been for John who is a gifted and dedicated news journalist for KUSI Television News in San Diego, several high impact stories would not have been told. I thank Tom Michaud who played a major role in my life and taught me the value of legacy in ways that even he doesn't know. To Allyson Hoover, who put up with my bouts of solitude, self-doubt, and travel related absences, I say, "Your uncompromising loyalty, encouragement and willingness to listen has meant more to me that you can know."

Thanks also to Nena Lucero whose invaluable assistance was a fantastic help and my editor Mark A. Clements, whose talent touches each of these pages.

TABLE OF CONTENTS

INTRODUCTION

LEGACY (noun): *Legacy is the memory imprint a person leaves behind at every step on the pathway of life's journey.*

Prepare yourself for a journey, because you're about to meet some of our nation's most successful people. "Success" is, of course, a slippery term. Many equate it with finances or notoriety—but being rich and/or famous is not a true measure of success, no matter how television and tabloids portray the "stars" of the day. What defines a successful life is *legacy*—what we leave behind; what we pass on to others.

When I started reaching out to people about contributing to this book, I sometimes had trouble contacting them at all. While most of these folks are extremely generous on various levels, they are also very much in demand. So some pay managers, handlers, assistants, and agents big bucks precisely to shield them from people like . . . well . . . me. But I'm pretty determined myself, and when I finally pierced those barriers and actually spoke to the person I sought, I was struck by an unexpected trait they all shared: humility. They were invariably surprised to learn that anyone might be interested in how they became the person they are.

As you'll discover in the pages that follow, these men and women also share another form of humility: a profound appreciation of the influence other people have had on them. Be it parents, members of the clergy, mentors, teachers or true friends, someone engendered a legacy by paving the way through love, encouragement and example.

Some of the contributors to this book overcame debilitating diseases or catastrophic injuries only to create organizations that help others heal, not just physically but mentally and emotionally. Others have taught, motivated, and inspired people through the examples of sheer hard work, determination and stubbornness of spirit. You will recognize the names of many these people as luminaries in theater, science, athletics or economics . . . who went on to use their fame as a tool for doing good works.

The names of other contributors will be less familiar, but not so the names and reputations of the organizations they founded, created, or to which they have dedicated their lives. Many of these contributors prefer to stay out of the spotlight while they dedicate themselves to their work and the people they serve.

Finally there are the contributors who are not famous at all, yet they live their lives with exemplary honor—heroism, even—as they reach out with kindness and compassion to touch the lives of others in small but meaningful ways.

All of the stories are told in the words of those who have lived them, making this book a unique blend of voices and experiences.

Some who read this book might, at first, believe that the legacy one creates is for tomorrow. It is my belief that legacy is about *now*. Every tomorrow is born of today, and as our lives brush against the lives of others, the impact can be felt forever.

That is the power of personal heroes . . . and the legacies they pass along.

THE PATHWAY OF LEGACY

Throughout our lives we meet, interact with, listen to, and exchange information with millions of people. Most often we glean from these occasions only what we need to serve our needs at the moment, then the memory is filed away or discarded. But every now and again the impact of what we experienced or learned is so important it's like an incredibly valuable object that we put away for safekeeping, to be brought out and admired when we need comfort—like a favorite photograph or a gift from someone special in our lives.

I call these experiences "Legacy Moments." Even very long spans of passing time do not diminish their shine or value.

Each of the men and women whose stories you are about to read either experienced such moments themselves, inspired such moments in others, or both. All are extraordinary people. I asked them to contribute their stories to this book not because of their political or religious leanings, or their motivations, but on the basis of their contributions to humanity. If that sounds like a lofty goal, I would agree—but "humanity" means, very simply, you and me and everyone we pass on the street every day. From our co-workers to the homeless person holding a sign up asking for change . . . *we* are humanity.

The folks who contributed stories about their mentors, influencers and personal heroes are, of course, "personal heroes" to me. Although they would probably be the last people to view themselves in that way, I know that when you read and understand their accomplishments and the way that they've touched the lives of others, you will agree with me.

What makes this book unique is that during my discussions with these individuals we talked not about *them* so much as about the people in their lives who touched, motivated and in many instances loved them—in other words, the people *they* looked up to as personal heroes. In all honesty, this was the first time many of them had been asked these questions, and in some cases they were forced to revisit memories they had buried long ago. Reliving the memories of our own experiences and recalling the people who helped make us who we are can be painful and bittersweet. Sharing such intimacies with a total stranger was a tremendous act of faith; I am forever in my contributors' debt for giving me that trust. I assure you that more than a few tears were shared along the journey of writing this book.

In an attempt to organize the stories that follow in a meaningful sequence, I have tried to define the particular kind of Legacy Moment each contributor is best remembered for or associated with. This proved to be the most challenging aspect of putting this book together, as these men and women have touched other peoples' lives on so many different levels. As you'll see, the categories are only generalizations; they in no way pigeonhole the accomplishments and legacies of each storyteller.

I offer this collection of stories to not only demonstrate that our world is full of amazing and giving people, but to inspire each of us to reach out, give of ourselves and strive to become, in whatever way we can, a Personal Hero.

PROLOGUE
The Photograph

Seligman, Arizona, is now more a memory than the thriving town it was half a century ago, when both the railroad and the famous highway Route 66 fed travelers through the little town's businesses, restaurants and hotels. It's certainly not the sort of place where I would have expected to experience either a vivid Legacy Moment brought to me by a remarkable man . . . or the intersection of the shadows of our two lives. (The fact that we never know when or with whom our lives will intersect is another reason to live our legacy.)

You might not recognize Frank Shankwitz's name, but you're familiar with his deeds. As he grasped my hand in greeting, I felt a deep and easy respect for this man whose eyes have seen more pain and courage than most people can imagine. His scarred and weathered face matched perfectly the well-worn cowboy hat that topped his short gray hair. Like the rugged, heroic figures we picture wearing the tin star of the Old West lawman, Frank spent the better part of four decades of his life serving and protecting the people of the state of Arizona while wearing the badge of the Highway Patrol. To many people, just being a law enforcement officer for that long makes him a hero. But to the hundreds of thousands of terminally ill children and their families whose lives Frank has touched as the founder of

Make-A-Wish Foundation, the word "hero" takes on a whole new meaning.

While I was researching the people I thought would make good candidates for a book focused on compassion, charity, success, and personal heroism, I figured Frank embodied all those qualities. This impression was reinforced the first time I contacted him and explained what I was trying to accomplish. Without hesitation he agreed to help by telling me the story of his personal heroes. But when I told him that, for his convenience, I'd be happy to drive down from my home in Las Vegas to meet him in Prescott where he lives, he said, "I'll save you some driving time," and suggested we meet in Seligman, Arizona, at a restaurant owned by a friend of his.

I admit I had to Google the town, which I'd never heard of before, but I was happy to oblige. I was even happier when I discovered that Seligman is located on old Route 66, a highway that not only defined an entire era to many Americans but one that holds a special place in my heart.

Although it's been more than a decade since the death of my father, I still find myself picking up the phone to dial his number from time to time. One of my earliest memories is of a photograph that hung on the wall of his room. He'd snapped it somewhere along Route 66 while he and my mother were traveling on the famous highway. Although my father fancied himself an artistic photographer, this particular picture didn't seem terribly remarkable: it showed a series of Old West-style storefronts with their characteristic square angles and the names of the business in Western lettering across the front. Still, the photo invoked powerful feelings of nostalgia in me. I'd seen it every day as I grew from child to man in the soft warmth of my family home, and

I can still feel the hot trails of the tears that crawled down my cheek when, yielding to the inevitable changes that follow death, I finally took the photo off the wall to pack away.

But the memories associated with it remained. The stories my parents told me about driving down Route 66 had had a powerful impact on my life. As a child I'd raptly watched the television series *Route 66*, named after the famous road—and thanks to modern technology I still watch it now. From the time I was old enough to drive until today my vehicle of choice has been the same car driven by the duo whose adventures were chronicled on the show: the quintessential Americans sports car, the Chevy Corvette convertible.

So when Frank suggested that we meet at his friend's restaurant on old Route 66, I smiled at the vision of myself cruising there with the top of my 'Vette down and the wind blowing through my hair.

I was not disappointed. After a wonderful drive I arrived in Seligman with plenty of time to spare. The town looked much the way I figured it had ever since the freeway system made Route 66 obsolete: a bit worn and tired, relying on the nostalgia of a simpler time for survival, yet humming along with the support of, or perhaps despite, its few modern structures. I found the restaurant and pulled into its parking lot, then left the Corvette's engine running while I viewed the old building's weathered exterior. Somehow I knew that inside, the coffee would be strong and the enticing smell of frying bacon would waft perpetually in the air.

Finally I stepped out of my car and did a couple of stretches to work the kinks out after the long drive—and that's when the Legacy Moment struck me so hard I literally had to grab my car for support. Directly across the street was a view that caused a collision of emotions inside me: I was looking at my father's photograph. Not just the same buildings, but the same angle and distance as in the photo I'd seen for most of my life.

I was standing exactly were my father had stood when he captured that image more than half a century before.

I remained there for quite a while, drinking in the view I now shared with the man whose love, wisdom, and humor lives on in my heart, as well as the flood of memories that erupted. Yes, I shed a few tears—but I figure that when fate reaches out and lays its hand on your shoulder and your heart, it's best to acknowledge that a wonder has occurred.

Finally I turned and walked into the restaurant, where I met a man whose own journey could easily fill volumes. As you read his story you'll understand why Frank chose this little town on a forgotten highway to tell me about his life and the hero who still inspires his heart.

As for me, I knew that our separate journeys were meant to intersect across the street from some old buildings captured in a photograph taken decades ago on historic Route 66.

The Legacy of
COMPASSION

*"Until he extends the circle of his compassion to all living
things, man will not himself find peace."*
— ALBERT SCHWEITZER

Life is a river of struggles dotted with occasional
triumphs. Each of us is given a unique set of
circumstances and challenges (including some of our
own making) to navigate down our life's journey. It is
understandably human to become caught up in our
own issues of relationships, health, loss, success, jobs
and family, to name a few. But even as crowded as our
lives are, there are men and women who stand out in
our memories for the impact they had on our lives, or
the life of someone who we love, or perhaps even the
life of a passing stranger. Whether their act was a small
gesture of kindness or an incredible feat of sacrifice, it
left an indelible mark because that person shared the
Legacy of Compassion.

"Why can't we do that for all the children?
Have them make a wish and then make it happen?"

FRANK SHANKWITZ

Who is Frank Shankwitz? Raised in northern Arizona, Frank Shankwitz joined the Arizona Department of Public Safety in 1972 and was assigned to the Arizona Highway Patrol as a car officer in Yuma. While there he worked with children as a coach for the Special Olympics program.

In 1975, Frank was transferred to the Phoenix area to be part of a new ten-man motorcycle tactical unit. For the next ten years, whenever Frank was assigned to small towns he would visit local grade schools, talk about bicycle safety, and let the children sit on his motorcycle.

Later, Frank was one of the primary officers from the Arizona Highway Patrol responsible for granting the "wish" of Chris, a seven-year-old boy with leukemia. Chris wanted to be a highway patrol motorcycle officer like his heroes, Ponch and John from the television show *CHiPs*. Before his death Chris was made the first and only honorary Arizona Highway Patrol officer in the history of the Arizona Highway Patrol, complete with a custom-made uniform, badge, and motor officer wings.

This experience inspired Frank to launch a nonprofit foundation that would let children "Make-A-Wish" and have it come true.

Currently a member of the Yavapai County Mounted Sheriff's Posse, Frank has 40 years of service in law enforcement. A feature film about his life entitled *Wish Man* is currently in production.

Frank and his wife, Kitty continue to reside in Prescott, Arizona. For more information please visit **www.wishman1.com**.

•••

M y story starts with my mother, who was born in Chicago in 1920. In 1940, after working in Arizona for two years as a Harvey Girl—a waitress trained to work in a line of restaurants that served train passengers across the United States—she returned to Chicago to take care of her mother, who was very ill with cancer. Not long after that my mother met and married my dad, but they divorced soon after I was born, and mom decided to return to Arizona. She never was much of a city gal.

I was not quite ten when we set off, heading through Michigan where my mother knew people and could work odd jobs. She'd get a job at a restaurant for a day or two, just long enough to earn enough gas money for us to move on. We lived in tents, we lived in the back of a car; we were kind of like the first homeless people. It took us three months to reach Arizona. Then, just outside the town of Williams, we literally ran out of money, gas and everything else. So, my mother pulled the car onto the property of an old ranch where she thought we could camp.

Williams is located up high in the mountains, and it was October or November. A light snowfall tried to get into our tent through rips in the sides. We had a campfire going but nothing to eat except a couple of slices of bread and some peanut butter and jelly. When my mother told me this, she started to cry.

That was when a big cowboy came riding up on a horse. I stared at him. "Hi," he said. "I'm Herman Polk, and I'm curious. I saw the smoke from your fire—what are you doing on my ranch?"

My mother cried harder. The cowboy looked down at her red, swollen eyes. "What's the matter?"

She managed to give him our sob story. He listened to the whole thing and then said, "You come with me."

We spent a couple of days living in Herman's ranch house. He fed us well—that was the first time I ever ate cowboy beans—and I helped him work in the barn with the horses. A few days into our stay with Herman he told my mom, "I have a brother in Seligman. I just talked to him. His wife is a motel maid and says there's a gal who just quit and they have an opening. You can work there if you go talk to the owners."

So he filled our car up with gas and we drove to Seligman, where my mom was hired immediately as a motel maid. But we still had no place to live. To our amazement, Herman's brother Tom told us we could stay in his house. It was a little two-bedroom, 700 square-foot place, already crowded with Tom, his wife and their two young boys. Still, they gave my mother and me a couple of pallets on the kitchen floor to sleep on, which was a lot better than a tent with holes in it. Plus we were getting fed.

I also got a job, washing dishes at the Whitehorse Café. Full time. At the age of ten. But I didn't mind. I was earning forty cents an hour, while my mother was getting fifty cents for each room she cleaned.

We stayed at the Polks' house until friends of theirs offered to give us an old camping trailer. It was pretty run-down, but they helped us fix it up, and we parked it behind the old motel and ran a hose into the motel for water and a cord for power. We couldn't afford to pay for hot water, so to take a shower I had to go to one of the big round houses belonging to the Santa Fe Railroad, where engineers would change shifts and put on new crew for the steep haul over the mountains. Because of all the steam production there, they allowed the local kids to use the showers.

One day while I was working at the café, I noticed a Mexican guy building a new structure nearby. I went over and said hi. He asked me my name.

"Frank Shankwitz."

"My name's Juan. Frank, how about you go on and grab a hammer and help me out?"

I did as he asked. I didn't have a father to teach me this stuff, after all.

"What are we building?" I asked.

"Oh, it's going to be the most famous drive-in restaurant on Route 66. The Snow Cap. When it's done I'll feed you one of the best hamburgers in Arizona, and something I invented called the Root Beer Freeze."

Although Juan was only in his late twenties, he became a father figure to me. My mother and I weren't making enough money to pay for both food and our bills, so the Mexican people in town kept bringing us beans and tortillas to keep us going. One day Juan told me, "All these people helping you and feeding you? Someday, when you can, give back. Help other people in need."

That was 1953, long before the term "give back" became popular. What he said made sense, but I didn't see how I could do it. Every penny I earned went straight to my mom. Eventually she got a job in Prescott, but it didn't pay terribly well either, and by then I was making enough money that she left me in Seligman for a year. I moved in with a widowed Mexican lady and her son—and again Juan preached to me. "This gal is helping you out, so even though you're paying a bit of room and board, make sure you do extra stuff for her. Give back to her."

So I cleaned her yard and kept everything in good repair.

Eventually I joined my mother in Prescott, where I graduated from high school. Then I joined the air force. Although this was during the Vietnam era I ended up in England, and afterward returned to Arizona and got a job at Motorola in Phoenix. I was studying engineering on the G.I. Bill, but despite the good pay and fine prospects, I got bored with living in the city. I was a product of Seligman and Prescott, and just didn't like the urban life.

Some friends of mine who had joined the Arizona Highway Patrol kept bugging me to do the same, so I applied and got accepted right away. Thanks to my little bit of college education I graduated almost at the top of the class and became very successful handling accident investigations.

In 1972, while still on probation, I was asked to join a new motorcycle division that had just started in Yuma. The squad consisted of ten guys working the entire state of Arizona.

Then in 1977 we went to work the town of Parker, Arizona, a little burg of six to seven hundred people situated on the Colorado River. During spring break the population would explode to fifty or sixty thousand drunken, stoned college kids celebrating.

Working Parker was like going to a war zone: twelve hour days for twenty to thirty days in a row. That particular year was especially bad: I got involved in the high speed pursuit of a drunk driver who had been running cars off the road. I was following close behind him when he hit a curb and flipped over at 70 miles per hour.

An instant later another driver struck me broadside and threw me across the road. Result: what we called a "963A—officer killed."

I was pronounced dead. One of the officers called in an ambulance, and after repeated attempts at CPR, radioed in that he couldn't revive me. Just then an off-duty emergency nurse who worked part time at a diner ran out and started CPR and heart massage on me . . . and after three and a half minutes, brought me back.

I learned this later, after going through what is called a "tunnel" in a death situation. The tunnel was completely black except that I saw my two daughters. Then the tunnel narrowed toward a light. It kept getting smaller . . . but then reversed and got larger and brighter until I was alive, awake, and felt something tickling my face. Then I realized something else was pressing against my lips, as if I were being kissed. My eyes opened and I saw the nurse, breathing into my mouth while her hair brushed across my face.

I thought, *If I'm in heaven, this is great.*

Then I heard guys in the background yelling, "She brought him back!"

I had no idea what they were talking about. But that was when the pain kicked in: my skull was fractured.

During the six months it took me to recover, I had to speak to a psychologist to make sure I was okay to go back to work. But I really only had one problem: I kept thinking, *Why was I spared? Why did God spare me on this?*

That accident changed my life, but I didn't realize how much, not then.

In 1980 I was on motorcycle duty when I got a call from dispatch in Phoenix telling me to get to the nearest phone. I drove to a gas station and called.

"There's this little seven-year-old boy named Chris," I was told. "He has leukemia and only has a couple of weeks to live. His heroes are Ponch and John from the TV show *CHiPs*."

I nodded. Every motorcycle cop knew that show.

"The department's going to set up a special day for him. We got permission from his mom and doctor to pick him up from the hospital in one of our helicopters and fly him to headquarters in Phoenix. The director wants you to be standing by there with a motorcycle when they land."

I knew this request was about more than me being a motorcycle officer. At the time I was on the fatal accident investigation team. That's all we investigated: fatal accidents, 24 hours a day. Which meant I was familiar with handling the dying, the dead, and the bereaved.

Then I got the good news. "You're authorized Code 2 from where you are into Phoenix." That meant I had permission to forget all the rules of the road in order to reach headquarters in time to greet the helicopter.

I was standing alongside my bike when the chopper landed. Two paramedics hopped out, followed by a little boy with a huge grin on his face. He ran over to me.

"Hi, I'm Chris," he said, and gave me a high-five. Then he stared at me like I was some kind of hero. "Can I sit on your motorcycle?"

"Sure." I lifted him up and was amused to see that he'd watched *CHiPs* so much he knew where all the controls were.

"Want to go for a ride?' I asked.

"No . . . ."

"Why not? You just rode in a helicopter!"

He lowered his eyes. "Helicopters have doors."

I would learn that even though Chris wanted to be a motorcycle officer, doors were very important to him. But just then one of our sergeants rolled up in a patrol car.

"How would you like to help drive that?" I asked.

"Great!"

I hoisted him onto the sergeant's lap. Chris was chewing bubble gum, and as the car started moving he grinned and blew a huge bubble toward me.

I turned to his mother. "Well, there's our bubble gum trooper." His mom would later write a book that's still in publication today: *The Little Bubble Gum Trooper.*

Later that day Chris went to our headquarters building, where the director of the Arizona Highway Patrol presented him with an official Smokey Bear officer's hat and his own official badge, which is still assigned to him to this day. Next he went to meet the director, who swore him in as the first and only honorary highway patrol officer in the history of the Arizona Highway Patrol. That was in 1980. It's now 2014 and he's still the only one.

Chris ran around laughing like any other seven-year-old rather than one with a fatal disease. When I looked at his mother she had tears in her eyes, and I knew she was seeing the same thing I was: *I got my little boy back.*

After the festivities, instead of returning to the hospital Chris was given permission by his doctor to go home. "His vitals are great," the doctor said. "I don't know what's going on."

After Chris left I turned to the sergeant and said, "We just made him a highway patrolman, but he doesn't have a uniform."

The sergeant agreed that that was improper. Back then highway patrol uniforms were custom-made in a little shop in Phoenix. Although it was closing time, the sergeant and I knocked on the door of the shop and told Chris's story to the gals inside. "He's seven years old and stands about this tall; could you make a uniform for him?"

They spent all night doing so. In the morning we picked it up and I, with the permission of our commander, led a caravan of motorcycles and highway patrol cars to Chris's neighborhood, red lights flashing and sirens whooping. When we presented Chris with his uniform he ran and put it on, then came back beaming. We all took pictures.

He asked me how he could become a highway patrol motor officer like me.

I grinned. "First you have to pass a riding test. You can do it in the driveway right now if you want."

He ran back to his room and returned riding the small electric motorcycle his mom had gotten him in place of a wheelchair. He wore his helmet, his little rubber boots, and a serious expression.

After he rode the course he said, "Did I pass the test?"

"Yes you did, Chris."

"Will I ever get one of these?" He reached up and touched the wing-shaped badge on my uniform.

"Yes you will." The wings had to be special ordered, so I went immediately to the jeweler who made them and told him the story of Chris. He said he could have the wings finished in a couple days. I figured that would work out well, because the doctor had allowed Chris to stay home for another day.

But I had just picked up the wings when I got a call saying "Code 2, find a pay phone right away." When I did, I was told that Chris had been returned to the hospital—in a coma.

When I got to his room I noticed his uniform hanging right by the bed. Chris lay there motionless, his mother sitting beside him. But as I pinned the wings on his uniform shirt he opened his eyes. He looked at me, then up at the wings on the shirt.

"Am I a motorcycle officer now?" he asked in a very small voice.

"Yes you are, Chris."

He sat up with a huge smile on his face and played with his uniform and wings for a while. He talked to his mom and seemed to have the greatest time. But then he got tired, went to sleep and slid back into a coma.

Chris passed away that evening. I always like to think that maybe those wings were, for him, comparable to heaven.

Not long afterward the director called me into his office. "We hear Chris is going to be buried in a small town outside Chicago. We lost a fellow officer. Will you and another officer go to make sure he gets a full police funeral?"

"Of course," I said.

"We can't pay for it and it's going to come out of your vacation time, but I already authorized for you to be in complete uniform the whole time."

"I'd be honored to go."

I started getting donations from the guys, and between both divisions we collected enough to pay for our airfare to Chicago and back. The Fraternal Order of Police in Chicago agreed to provide transportation from Chicago to the town of Kewanee, Illinois.

Chris was buried in his uniform beneath a marker that read *Chris Gracious, Arizona Trooper.*

The affair received press coverage everywhere we went; then ABC picked it up, and suddenly it was a national story. Everybody was interested in this little boy. But I felt there had to be more to it than this. As I was flying back to Arizona I kept thinking, *This little boy wished to be a motorcycle officer like Ponch and John, and we made it happen. Why can't we do that for all the children? Have them make a wish and then make it happen?*

And that's how the Make-A-Wish Foundation was born.

I had finally figured out how to do what Juan had taught me when I was ten years old: give back. This was my purpose. This was why God had spared me when I died in that crash. I might not have enough money to grant wishes on my own, but there were other ways I could make it work.

It took six months for me to get the right people involved and start collecting donations. In March of 1981 we granted our first official wish, which went to another seven-year-old boy dying of leukemia. He wanted three things: to grow up and become a fireman, to go to Disneyland, and to ride in a hot air balloon. It so happened that a friend of mine had a brother who was a fireman, so that part was easy to arrange. The Phoenix Fire Department fitted the boy out with an entire uniform, including a coat and helmet, and let him slide down the pole. He was nothing but smiles.

I also knew someone who owned a hot air balloon, so we took care of that for him as well. Disney was a different matter. When I called them, they hung up on me. After all, we were brand new and they had never heard of us. When my wife called they wouldn't listen to her, either.

I got back on the phone and asked to speak with the director of Public Relations.

"This is the Arizona Highway Patrol," I said. "We have a warrant for one of your guys."

That got the director on the phone. I recited my name and badge number and those of my supervisor, then admitted I'd lied about the warrant. "I could be terminated for saying that," I admitted, then gave him the story about the boy with leukemia.

He told me not to worry, they'd take care of everything, and to this day Disney is one of the biggest supporters of Make-A-Wish. They had one of their people with Chris during his entire visit, making sure that he got the royal treatment. The Anaheim Fire Department sent two fire trucks to pick him and his mom up from the airport, then let the boy ride in the back of one of the trucks as they drove to the hotel. Two paramedics stayed with him all day in case he needed them for any medical issues. At the Disney Park they drove him straight to the front entrance, and later returned him to the airport in the fire trucks.

That was just the start, of course. Since the inception of Make-A-Wish 33 years ago, more than 300,000 children worldwide have had their wishes granted. That's comes to one wish granted every 33 minutes somewhere in the world. We have 63 chapters in the US and 36 international chapters on five continents. When you include the families of the children, the foundation has affected over a million people . . . and all because of one little boy who wanted to be a highway patrol motorcycle officer . . . and a highway patrol motorcycle officer who had been taught the importance of paying back.

"That role opened my eyes to a whole other aspect of what happens to people who go to war."

GARY SINISE

Who is Gary Sinise? For over thirty years, Gary Sinise has stood as an advocate of America's servicemen and women. It began in the early '80s with his support of Vietnam veterans groups and the creation of Vet's Night, a program offering free dinners and performances to veterans at the Steppenwolf Theatre in Chicago. His commitment continued into the '90s, working on behalf of the Disabled American Veterans organization which he continues to actively support. Since the attacks of September 11, 2001, his dedication to our nation's active duty defenders, veterans and first responders has become a tireless crusade of support, service and gratitude to all those who protect our freedom and serve our country.

His portrayal of Lt. Dan Taylor in the landmark film *Forrest Gump* formed an enduring connection with servicemen and women throughout the military community. After several USO handshake tours in 2003, Sinise formed the "Lt. Dan Band" in early 2004 and began entertaining troops serving at home and abroad. The band now performs close to 50 shows a year for military bases, charities and fundraisers supporting wounded warriors, Gold Star families, veterans and troops around the world.

Sinise serves as spokesperson for both the American Veterans Disabled for Life Memorial Foundation and Disabled American Veterans, and was instrumental in raising funds for the Pentagon Memorial in Washington, D.C., and the Brooklyn Wall of Remembrance in NYC. He serves on executive councils for the Medal of Honor Foundation and the USO, and is an advisory board member for Hope for the Warriors. In recognition of his humanitarian work on behalf of our troops and veterans, Mr. Sinise has received many distinguished awards including the Bob Hope Award for Excellence in Entertainment from the Medal of Honor Society, the Spirit of the USO Award, and the Ellis Island Medal of Honor. In 2008 he was a recipient of the Presidential Citizens Medal, the second-highest civilian honor awarded to citizens for exemplary deeds performed in service of the nation, only the third actor ever to receive this honor. In 2012, Sinise was presented with the Spirit of Hope Award by the Department of Defense and was named an honorary chief petty officer by the navy.

In 2011, to expand upon his individual efforts, Sinise established the Gary Sinise Foundation. Its mission is to serve and honor our nation's defenders, veterans, first responders, their families and those in need by creating and supporting unique programs that entertain, educate, inspire, strengthen and build communities.

Through its Building for America's Bravest™ partnership, the Gary Sinise Foundation is building custom Smart Homes for severely wounded veterans. Additionally, the foundation has created programs such as Serving Heroes to serve hearty meals for deploying troops; Invincible Spirit Festivals to boost the morale and spirits of the patients, their families and the medical staff at military hospitals; and the Gary Sinise Foundation Relief & Resiliency Outreach dedicated to assisting those in urgent need. It has also partnered with GE on GetSkillstoWork.org, a program designed to help veterans put their military experience to use in civilian jobs.

Giving back to those who sacrifice for our nation and encouraging others to do the same has become Gary Sinise's personal quest and what he hopes will endure as a legacy of service to others. "Freedom and security are precious gifts that we, as Americans, should never take for granted," says Sinise. "We must do all we can to extend our hand in times of need to those who willingly sacrifice each day to provide that freedom and security. While we can never do enough to show our gratitude to our nation's defenders, we can always do a little more."

For more information please visit **www.garysinisefoundation.org**.

•••

I grew up south of Chicago in a town called Blue Island, Illinois. In 1963 we moved to Highland Park, where my mom was a homemaker and my father an editor in the film business. He worked mostly on commercials and industrial films in Chicago, and was one of the first independent editors to start his own business.

My father served in the Navy in the early '50s. His father was a WWI veteran, and his two brothers served in WWII. There were a lot of veterans in my family, but as a young person I didn't pay attention to that. I was attending high school during the winding down of the Vietnam War. I didn't pay too much attention to that then, either, although my parents were concerned that the war would extend and I'd be drafted into it. At that time, the early '70s, the Vietnam War was tearing the country apart.

But I was more interested in rock 'n' roll. I'd been playing in bands since I was in fourth grade, but in high school I was rocking out with my own band, playing Led Zeppelin, the Who, that kind of thing.

One day in 1971 I was hanging out in the school hallway when the drama teacher walked up and asked me to audition for *West Side Story*. For the hell of it I tried out, and I got into the show—and that event, basically accidental, started me down the acting road.

I found being on stage really exciting, so I kept auditioning for shows and kept getting in. I met some really great people, including one of my best friends, Jeff Perry, who's now on a TV show called *Scandal*. He, another friend named Terry Kinney, and I ended up starting Steppenwolf Theatre Company in Chicago. That theater is 40 years old now. It's also where I met a young actress, Moira Harris, who became my wife.

Moira's two brothers served in Vietnam, and her sister joined the army out of college, became a captain and married a Vietnam veteran who stayed in the army for about 22 years. Through Moira's brothers I learned quite a bit about the Vietnam experience and their time at war. One of the brothers had been a helicopter pilot, and the other a West Point graduate who went to 'Nam the first time as a platoon leader and then again as company commander.

The stories they told me were what first woke me to the problems Vietnam veterans faced and have had to endure ever since. It occurred to me that when I was a kid playing hockey and drinking beer and doing plays and not really paying attention to anything else, guys not much older than I was were going through nightmarish experiences in the jungles of Southeast Asia—and then coming home only to be treated terribly.

At about that same time, 1980, I was the artistic director for Steppenwolf Theatre and looking around for plays to do. I read about a play called *Tracers* being put on in Los Angeles. It had been written by a group of Vietnam veterans who got together and chose this way to exorcize some of the demons that were still haunting them from their military experience. They talked about their experiences and assembled a series of vignettes into something they could put on stage.

I flew out to LA to see the play, and it knocked me out. I begged them to let me direct it in Chicago with my company. They eventually granted me the rights, and I made it my mission to do the play properly and honestly for all the Vietnam veterans.

I was passionate about telling these stories, partly in honor of all my wife's family members who had served in the military. Not long after the play opened at my theater, Moira's older brother passed away from cancer, making it all the more compelling to me to tell the story of the Vietnam veteran, to honor my wife's brother and the many Vietnam veterans whose stories were not getting told.

I was very motivated. Every Tuesday night we'd have a Veteran's Night in which we filled the theater with veterans—mostly Vietnam veterans, since of course it was their story being told on stage. They were a part of our society, but thanks to the temper of the nation at the time they served, when they returned from war they had to just disappear into the background. Nobody wanted to hear their stories then, but now they could see their stories being performed right before their eyes. It was a healing experience which became more than just actors doing a play.

As the director, I was motivated to whip my actors into shape and make them as passionate about telling these stories as I was. It became very cathartic, and Vet's Night has lived on for 30 years now. Since 1984, every dress rehearsal has been a night for veterans. My foundation began sponsoring that event at the Geffen Playhouse, and now for every dress rehearsal they bring in a group of Veterans and give them a free meal and a free show.

Through the 1980s I was very focused on veterans' issues. I helped build a Vietnam veterans Memorial in Lansing, Illinois, and as an actor had the opportunity to audition for the role of a Vietnam veteran in a movie entitled *Forrest Gump*. I wanted to do it very badly, and luckily got the part.

That role opened my eyes to a whole other aspect of what happens to people who go to war: those who come back disabled and injured. I wanted to know about that experience so I could play my role in *Forrest Gump* as accurately as possible. After the movie came out I established a connection with the DAVA, the Disabled American Veterans Association, which goes back 20 years working with the wounded and supporting injured veterans. Then, after 9/11 when the US started to deploy to Iraq and Afghanistan, it became clear that there was a role for me to play for our active duty folks as well—so I started volunteering.

After 9/11 I was frightened and very troubled. It's stayed with me ever since. Between that, the veterans in my own family, and having met Vietnam veterans who've gone through some very serious things, I formed a clear mission: as a public figure I wanted to shine a light on those who serve our country and sometimes pay a very heavy price. I've met a lot of people who have motivated me to use what I have—the spotlight and the megaphone and the microphone—to shed light on those who have sacrificed so much for the rest of us. I want to help ensure that what happened to our Vietnam veterans does not happen to veterans returning from Iraq and Afghanistan.

All of this came together in the Gary Sinise Foundation. I've always felt that service to others is a gift and a reward, and the more I've done it, the more spiritual I've become. Once I found out that taking action really can make a difference in the world, how could I not do it?

I've always been somebody who doesn't like a lot of chitchat, a lot of talk. I think if you're going to do something, you do it. Having the role as Lieutenant Dan in *Forest Gump* is an example. There was some sort of God's blessing on that situation because there I was, a guy who was passionate about the military and military families, and I just happened to play an injured veteran in a movie everyone seems to have seen multiple times.

The military and the veterans' communities really embraced the story of that character. Lieutenant Dan's story in *Forest Gump* is one of resilience. He wants to be a great leader and a great soldier; he wants to serve and do right by his men. But after he marches his men into a little valley were they're ambushed and killed and he loses his legs, he carries survivor's guilt and harbors resentment towards Forrest for saving his life instead of letting him die with the rest of his men. He can't forgive Forrest for that until the end of the story when he realizes there's still life ahead for him. There's life after Vietnam and what happened in the valley that day.

So Lieutenant Dan moves on. In the end he's successful; he's standing up, he's married, he has a new life, he's a successful businessman. That's how we'd like the story to end for all our military veterans who have trouble recovering from war. We want them to recover—and if I can do something through my foundation to help them mend from what they've gone through in the defense of freedom, the freedom you and I benefit from, I feel I'm serving my country!

Earlier I mentioned my brother-in-law, Lieutenant Boyd McCanna Harris, the West Point graduate who went to Vietnam and returned to teach at West Point. He rose to the rank of lieutenant colonel before getting cancer and passing away at the age of thirty-nine.

I've met generals—three- and four-star generals—who knew him, men who were a little younger than him at West Point and who studied under him. Many of these leaders felt that if my brother-in-law had lived he would have risen in the ranks and become a great general.

So when I went to work on Lieutenant Dan, I thought, Well, *that's* Lieutenant Dan. We created a backstory for the character. He graduated from the Virginia Military Institute, he wanted to be a great officer, and his vision for his future was to rise in the ranks—just the way my brother-in-law was doing before he passed away.

There was another family connection in Lieutenant Dan as well. If you see the movie you'll notice that when Dan has his shirt off there are dog tags around his neck—those are actually the dog tags of my wife's brother-in-law. His name was Jack Treese, and he was a combat medic in the service for 22 years. He wore those dog tags in Vietnam, and I wore them in the movie.

What I did in *Forrest Gump*, and what I hope to do with my foundation and my traveling, is to remind people of the importance of what our military veterans have done. I want all our citizens to understand how necessary it is to express appreciation and gratitude to anyone who serves in the armed forces, and to reach out to them if they're having trouble. When I travel around the country I always urge people to find their local veterans. You might find someone who's had multiple deployments to Iraq and Afghanistan and is isolating him- or herself, and needs a helping hand. These veterans have gone through a lot for us. We've been at war for a dozen years now, and that's a long time—we ask a lot of this military.

I hope my foundation will also be around for a long time, as a reliable resource offering reputable programs that address the needs of our veterans, first responders and others who put their lives on the line for our freedom, security and protection. I try to encourage and to inspire as many people as possible to take action. Set an example of service above self. Give, and you will indeed receive in return when you see the faces of those military children and those wounded veterans.

*"Paying attention to human potential and honoring each
person's journey is what existence is all about."*

BONNIE CARROLL

Who is Bonnie Carroll? Bonnie Carroll is the president and founder of the Tragedy Assistance Program for Survivors (TAPS), the national Veterans Service Organization that provides peer-based emotional support, grief and trauma resources and information, casualty casework assistance and crisis intervention for all those affected by the death of a loved one serving in, or in support of, the armed forces.

Ms. Carroll currently serves on the Department of Veterans Affairs Advisory Committee on Disability Compensation, the Board of Directors of the Association of Death Education and Counseling, and the Department of Defense Military Family Readiness Council. She recently co-chaired the DOD Task Force on the Prevention of Suicide in the Armed Forces.

Ms. Carroll served in Baghdad, Iraq, as the deputy senior advisor for programs in the Ministry of Communications. In that capacity she managed the execution of a quarter billion dollars in US supplemental funds for the reconstruction of the telecommunications capability in Iraq, the modernization of the postal service, and creation of the Iraq Communications and Media Commission. She continues to work with Iraqi families facing traumatic loss.

Before going to Iraq, Ms. Carroll was appointed to be the White House liaison for the VA in Washington, D.C. Prior to that she served as director of the Tragedy Assistance Program for Survivors (TAPS) and ensured the development of programs to aid families coping with a traumatic loss in the military.

Ms. Carroll founded TAPS following the death of her husband, Brigadier General Tom Carroll, in an army C-12 plane crash in 1992. She is a trained Critical Incident Stress Debriefer, member of the International Society for Traumatic Stress Studies and the American Association for Death Education and Counseling. She has authored numerous articles on grief and trauma and appeared on CNN, FOX, NBC's *The Today Show* and other programs, speaking about military loss. Ms. Carroll was featured in *People Magazine*'s "Heroes Among Us" and received recognition as Washingtonian of the Year. She also received the National Citizen for 2010 award from the Military Chaplains Association.

Ms. Carroll is a major in the Air Force Reserve, where she has served as chief, casualty operations, HQ USAF. Her last assignment was on the HQ USAF National Security and Emergency Preparedness staff in the Pentagon, and the USAF Directorate of Homeland Security. Prior to joining the USAFR, Major Carroll served 16 years in the Air National Guard as a transportation officer, logistics officer, and executive officer.

During her earlier career in Washington, D.C., Ms. Carroll lived and worked on Capitol Hill as a political consultant on presidential and congressional campaigns and lobbyist on aerospace and defense issues. In the federal government she held presidential appointments in the Reagan and Bush administrations, including a senior level position within the West Wing of the White House as executive assistant for Cabinet Affairs. In this capacity, she served as liaison for President Reagan with his cabinet, coordinating domestic and economic policy implementation. In the previous Bush administration, Ms. Carroll served in the White House Counsel's Office, assisting with the legal review process for presidential nominees to the cabinet and other senior government positions requiring Senate confirmation.

Ms. Carroll holds a degree in Public Administration and Political Science from American University and a degree in Equine Science from Springfield College. She has completed Harvard University John F. Kennedy School of Government's Executive Leadership Program on International Conflict Resolution, and is a graduate of several military service schools, including the USAF Logistics Officer Course, Squadron Officers School, Defense Equal Opportunity Management Institute, Academy of Military Science (Distinguished Graduate), and USAF Basic Training (Honor Graduate).

For more information please visit **www.taps.org**.

•••

I've been fortunate to work with many extraordinary individuals, starting with Ronald Reagan. I worked in the West Wing of the White House during his presidency, and couldn't have asked for a finer leader. Although toward the end of his administration there was a lot of talk about how he was suffering from the onset of Alzheimer's, to those who worked with him he was brilliant and sharp. He was involved in everything that was happening in this country, to bringing out the best in everyone on his team, and to making this country a better place. He believed that the government was there to serve the people.

One night he came by my office and said, "Bonnie, you're in the National Guard, aren't you?"

"Yes," I said. "One weekend a month, that's where I go to serve."

"There's something on television involving whales stuck in the ice that involves the National Guard," he said. "It's captured the imagination of the country. Everyone is pulling for these whales. Is there anything we can do to help? Call someone you know, but not the Pentagon because I don't want them up all night working on this."

Call someone quietly and see how we can help. That was classic Ronald Reagan: see how the federal government can engage and make a difference.

So I called someone I knew in the Guard, which led me to another person and another person and another person until I finally got the field office of the whale rescue effort way up in Barrow, Alaska. Colonel Tom Carroll was in command, but at first he couldn't take the call from the White House because he was out on the ice. It wasn't until two in the morning back in Washington that the colonel finally returned my call. I was still in my office in the West Wing, and we discussed the whale issue. "On behalf of the president," I said, "is there anything the federal government can do to support this?"

He got me up to speed on what was happening up there . . . and in the course of the conversation we suddenly felt we *knew* each other. It was a surreal experience. We both said, "Where have you been?" because we felt a bond so deep it seemed like just a continuation of an established relationship. And in fact, from that moment on we were together.

Tom was a man of tremendous vision. He looked at the whale rescue from a global perspective, as an opportunity to bring together not just the National Guard but the oil companies, Greenpeace—which is ordinarily at odds with both the oil companies and the military—and the Native Alaskans up in Barrow who had a very deep, spiritual connection with these whales.

Then the colonel asked the president to bring in the Soviets. Now, this was in the 1980s at the height of the Cold War, so to invite the Soviets to enter US waters was quite a big deal. But we did it. Then the colonel was flown over to a Soviet icebreaker on a US Army helicopter. Think about it: a US military helicopter landing on a Soviet vessel during the Cold War—and Tom and the Soviet captain, side by side, riding that icebreaker into US waters.

That was the kind of man Tom was: someone who looked at what we can do to change the world, how we could take a little circumstance and bring people from different cultures and viewpoints together and inspire them to accomplish things. That icebreaker broke through more than just ice; it cut through a barrier that had been created. And that's how the whales were freed.

Shortly after that, the Berlin Wall came down and all sorts of things started happening. Clearly the whale rescue didn't directly impact that, but it was among the first steps in the "thawing of the Cold War," and a beautiful, collaborative effort.

Tom and I soon married and became a team. It was humbling for me to watch Tom engage with his soldiers and inspire them to excel and become strong leaders, to live full lives, proud of who they were as people, soldiers, and as family men and women. He created a program for the National Guard called the Youth Core Challenge to take high school dropouts and give them the chance to join a six-month program during which they'd get healthy, sleep and eat well, become physically fit, and live in a safe environment away from gangs and off the street. Many kids came out of that program and went on to do great things. They came out as successes, with their GEDs and a little bit of money in their pockets, with vocational skills and a chance for better lives. That's what Tom was about. He was about honoring the individual and inspiring us all to do better.

Because of my connections in the West Wing, Tom and I had the chance to go back to Washington and meet socially with the Secretary of Defense and the Secretary of Veterans Affairs. Tom provided insight from the perspective of the soldier, which set the stage for some of the work that was done in the Gulf War. I don't think anyone knows that those plans were partially a result of Tom's inspiration.

He taught me that paying attention to human potential and honoring each person's journey is what existence is all about. Tom attained the rank of general officer in his early forties, the youngest army general pinned at that time, and was recognized by Colin Powell, then the chairman of the Joint Chiefs of Staff.

Tom was the son of a major general who had been killed in an army plane crash when Tom was just fifteen. His life was shaped by his father's service. After high school he enlisted in the army and went to Vietnam. He entered as a private, the lowest rank, and came out of Vietnam a captain. The only time he returned stateside was to go to officer school. He didn't have a college education; he was commissioned based on his experience and leadership. He finally finished college as a colonel, as a prerequisite to getting promoted to general.

To get his bachelor's degree Tom took some of the graduate record exams, including one to earn a credit for sociology. Tom never studied for it, but passed with flying colors because it was the study of the human condition that he had intuitively known and exemplified throughout his life. But he was so fascinated by the subject that even after passing the exam he bought some textbooks and started studying sociology. It just proved out the things he lived, the things he was already about: leading soldiers to be extraordinary individuals and mentoring them to be inspiring leaders, but also considering the human condition globally, and how something as seemingly trivial as a whale rescue can change the view of the Soviet Union.

Tom and I had a great life together. We had three teenagers, including two foster children we had taken in. One was Tom's stepdaughter. They were very busy and I was still in the National Guard and working full-time at the district attorney's office, and Tom was active as the deputy commissioner of Military and Veterans Affairs for the state of Alaska and leading the Alaska Army National Guard.

We were also engaged in the community. I got involved in victim/witness coordination and began working with a group called COPS, which stands for Concerns of Police Survivors, and another group called Victims for Justice. So life was full of being active in the community, raising a family with kids who had come from troubled lives, and loving each other. The kids were incredibly happy to be in that safe place. We had horses and were outdoors and loving Alaska; it was just the absolute, most ideal life I could ever dream of.

All that was shattered in a moment on November 12, 1992, when Tom's plane crashed into a mountain with seven other soldiers. All eight were killed, and everything came apart. In the aftermath I struggled to honor Tom's legacy and continue his vision of changing the world—not only within our family, but for all those who have suffered a loss in the military. But it was terribly difficult. There was relative peacetime in 1992. We'd been in and out of the Gulf War, but America still hadn't focused on the issue of death in the armed forces. Coming together with others who had suffered a loss in the military was a challenge. I went to some of the support groups like COPS, but they didn't resonate. They didn't understand the military; the members were all waiting for trials or looking for some other resolution to their journey.

I finally realized that there simply was no organization in this country to network surviving families in the military. There were some social groups: Gold Star Wives, Society of Military Widows, associations that military widows could join; but there was nothing that dealt with trauma of the first hours and days and months after a loss; the trauma and grief that children struggle with when they lose a parent in such a public and dramatic manner.

So over the next two years I created TAPS, the Tragedy Assistance Program for Survivors—with my husband as my inspiration throughout it all. It was an organization that would provide peer-based support, comfort and resources to others who had lost loved ones. I didn't think the Defense Department would embrace TAPS; I figured they'd say there was no need for another group. But when I showed them our little round logo with the folded flag and the missing man formation, they said, "This is wonderful," and thought that it had been around forever. They assumed TAPS had always existed.

I felt Tom's guidance through the process, knowing the things he would have done for his soldiers. I wanted to do it in his honor and as his legacy.

Over the past twenty years, TAPS has grown to be the partner of the Defense Department and the military; it's embraced by all the casualty officers and commanders. When they knock on a door and present that folded flag, they tell the family, "You are not alone. There are others there for you at TAPS who will walk this journey with you."

The theme of TAPS is "Remember the love, celebrate the life, and share the journey." It's not about the moment of death, whether due to hostile action or cancer or a motorcycle accident. It's about the life that was lived and the fact that their loved one stepped forward and raised his or her right hand and said "I will dedicate my life in selfless service to this nation."

It is now our honor and privilege to care for all the people that service member loved and left behind. To embrace them, comfort them and give them the resources and family to be there forever.

That's Tom's legacy.

KAREN GUENTHER

Who is Karen Guenther? Karen Guenther, the wife of an active duty United States Marine Corps colonel and a registered nurse with more than two decades of professional experience, is founder, president, and CEO of the Semper Fi Fund, a nonprofit organization supporting the men and women of the United States Armed Forces and their families. From its humble beginnings in 2004 as a locally based grassroots effort, the Semper Fi Fund has grown to a worldwide charitable organization that has distributed over $69 million in grants to service members and their families.

Under Karen's leadership, the Semper Fi Fund has been recognized as one of the premier non-governmental organizations supporting service members and their families. The fund continues to and has consistently earned the highest marks from the charitable industries' foremost and well-respected regulators—earning both an A+ rating from Charity Watch, and four stars from Charity Navigator.

Karen's work with the Semper Fi Fund has earned accolades including the US Field Artillery Association Molly Pitcher Award, the Marine Corps League Dickey Chapelle Award, the Daughters of the American Revolution Medal of Honor, and the Cookie Award from *Cookie Magazine* for mothers who make a difference in the world.

For more information please visit **www.semperfifund.org**.

•••

I grew up on a farm outside Caruthers, California, a town so small and rural I'm not even sure it can be found on a map. We raised grapes and kept horses and cows. After high school I went off to college at Fresno State and Cal Poly, but when my mom got sick with lupus I transferred to California State University at Fresno in order to be closer to home.

My parents were my greatest source of inspiration throughout my life. I watched them take care of others. They gave back to the community and to our family, always taking care of their brothers and sisters. When workers came up from Mexico, my mom would cook for them and made sure they weren't hungry, and my dad would give just about anybody the shirt off his back if they needed it. Our world was farming, so I watched him take care of those who worked with the grapes. He was also very involved in church; when the electricity there failed late at night he went to fix it so the church could have services the next day. He did many small things like that. For example, we had a cabin in the mountains. In winter my dad loved to drive around in his pickup truck and use the winch on the front to pull peoples' stuck vehicles out of snowbanks.

So I had two beautiful role models. When you grow up with that kind of influence, wanting to help the people in front of you is something you do subconsciously.

As I got older, Mother Teresa became another role model. I read almost every book that has ever been written about her. I was inspired by her love and caring; although she was a Catholic, she went to India and cared for Hindus. I was impressed by her love for mankind despite race, color, or religion; just mankind, the homeless, children living on the streets. When I was asked in college to write about who inspired me, I wrote about Mother Teresa. Like her, I believe the greatest gift of life is to help one another through it.

Because of the influence of my mother and father and Mother Teresa, I hope I will always be there to serve others—because that's my hope for the future, for our children. I have one daughter, and although we don't talk about it, she sees my husband's service as well: he's in active duty in the marines. We believe that our actions teach our daughter more than words ever could.

In college I dated a young man named Delmar, who planned to go into the air force. He had his pilot's license and was just full of life. On our first date he picked me up and flew me to a cute breakfast place. On the way back he put the plane through rolls and spins, and I wanted to do more. I loved flying with him.

One morning he called to invite me flying, but I couldn't go—I had to study for a test. Ordinarily I would have claimed to have a fever if it meant skipping out on studying to go flying, but that day I stayed home with my books. Delmar said he'd take a friend with him instead, and they'd buzz my house. When they did, Mom and I ran outside and waved up at the plane.

A moment later we heard the engine sputtering. The plane went into a spin and crashed in our horse pasture. It exploded, killing Delmar and his friend instantly.

One of the policemen who came to the site asked me to tell Delmar's parents what had happened—and I did. I went through that terrible experience with his folks, and although I didn't realize it at the time, that incident marked a moment in my life that would change me forever.

But it took another close call to make me realize just how much had changed. Not long after Delmar's death I attended a wedding out in the country with my friend Laura. It got late, and I decided to go home with some other friends. Later, Laura, driving along that same road, fell asleep at the wheel. Her car crossed the road and hit a tree, and Laura was killed. My purse was in the car with her; I was supposed to ride home with her that night.

Although at the time I was only in my early twenties, I learned just how precious life is.

I was majoring in plant pathology and intended to continue working with grapes, agriculture and horticulture. But after going through the bereavement process with Delmar's family and then Laura's, the course of my life shifted. I felt drawn to helping people who are going through trauma and crises. Perhaps it was a way of healing myself, but suddenly working in a vineyard didn't seem like something I wanted to do anymore. So I went to nursing school and became an intensive care unit emergency room nurse.

That job gave me plenty of opportunities to experience dealing with death and loss—but not until I married a marine did the ideas become personal again. The war in Iraq had begun, and suddenly my husband and thousands of other marines were marching to Baghdad. When those of us who stayed behind said goodbye to our loved ones at the San Diego Harbor, we weren't sure we would ever see them again—especially with all the talk of weapons of mass destruction that was floating around. It was a very scary time, but we spouses were a strong group. We supported each other.

When the first group of personnel returned from Iraq I was working at Balboa Naval Hospital in Camp Pendleton, and was invited to welcome back the arriving flight. A young wife—she looked seventeen or eighteen—was standing beside me when her husband appeared, sitting in a wheelchair. He had been severely injured and required an emergency craniotomy, so his face was distorted and swollen as they wheeled him from the back room. She hadn't seen him until that moment—and she started to pass out.

I grabbed her and held her up. Her husband was watching her face. "You can do this," I whispered in her ear. "I'm here for you, you can do this."

That was when it hit me: we had a lot of work to do, those of us who stayed behind. Many of our service members were no more than twenty years old, yet they were coming back wounded, and their families were going to need help.

That was the beginning of the Semper Fi Fund.

It started organically. I simply picked up the phone, called friends in my neighborhood and told them what I was seeing in the hospital. They jumped to action. At first we were short-sighted and planned to help only those on the first flights, but we ended up meeting every flight. We brought the families food, found them hotels and transportation—whatever they needed. We brought clean socks and toothbrushes to the wounded. We sat on the floor with them until two in the morning or until a family member showed up so they wouldn't be alone.

I think we all believed that after the marines came back from that particular deployment our work would be done. But now, almost 10 years later, we're still doing it. We started with a budget of $500—a hundred dollars from each of our personal bank accounts. But as word about what we were doing spread, other people asked to help. Our first donation was from Christian Lighthouse Church for $5,000. At the time we had three wounded Marines, and gave them all the money. It might have been a bad decision, but we did help those three families.

After that we just kept going, and more and more people wanted to be a part of it. Semper Fi became a way for Americans to pitch in. They saw on TV what was happening, and since they couldn't be there to help the military personnel directly, they could participate by helping service families.

None of this was due to me; all I did was listen. We had help from everybody. Our lawyer paid out of his own pocket to incorporate the organization. In fact, all along the way we had heroes helping our small group of spouses. We weren't MBAs. I'd taken exactly one business class in college, and dropped it because I didn't like it—now I wish I'd paid more attention! No, we've been blessed to be surrounded by people who *do* have the needed expertise—accountants, lawyers; it takes all of us to make this organization work.

In fact, it truly takes a village. From that $500 beginning, Semper Fi has grown into an international nonprofit with funding of 82 million dollars used to support 10,500 service members and their families. But we're still just as passionate and dedicated as we were in the days we were handing out toothbrushes and socks.

I've watched burnout happen in hospitals and with ICU nurses, and I've always been worried about that happening with our team. We take calls at two a.m.; we sit with family members as they watch their loved ones being taken off life support—it's as up-close and personal as you can get with trauma and crisis. But I haven't seen any burnout. Our people just keep going—I think because the act of service keeps them motivated.

These people—ordinary, dedicated and caring people like my parents—are my heroes today.

"Can you tell me the difference between being a good cop . . . and a great cop?"

RANDY SUTTON

Who **is Randy Sutton?** Randy's police career spanned three decades before he retired as a field lieutenant with the Las Vegas Metropolitan Police Department. To this day he remains recognized as one of the most highly decorated officers in department history, with numerous awards for lifesaving, exemplary service and valor. He is also one of America's best-known officers, having been featured on the popular reality show *COPS*, *America's Most Wanted*, and in films such as *Casino*, *Fools Rush In* and *Miss Congeniality II*, as well as appearances on television network and cable news as a commentator and a regular panelist on the television show *Fired Up*.

Randy is also the critically-acclaimed author of four books: *True Blue: Police Stories by Those Who Have Lived Them; A Cop's Life; True Blue: To Protect and Serve;* and *The Power of Legacy*. He has also written extensively for national magazines on the topics of ethics, integrity and leadership.

Randy is the creator of THEPOWEROFLEGACY.COM, a website dedicated to encouraging the principles of honor, integrity, compassion and kindness—subjects he speaks about passionately to law enforcement and civic/business organizations across the country. He is also the founder and president of CELEBRATING LEGACY, a company where "Memories Live Forever," providing members with the ability to celebrate lives in the present, honor lives from the past, and share family histories for the future.

For more information please visit **www.thepoweroflegacy.com** and **www.celebratinglegacy.com**.

•••

In 1896, Alfred Nobel, the inventor of dynamite, would leave a legacy known throughout the world: he would use his vast fortune to create something that came to symbolize and celebrate the greatest scientific and social achievements in the twentieth century and beyond. Today, the Nobel Peace Prize is considered one of history's greatest achievements, and the idea behind its development has lived on through many generations.

Without a doubt the financial rewards to the recipients of Mr. Nobel's grand plan add fuel to the idea that brought about its birth, but Nobel's true legacy is not his tremendous wealth: it lies in the ideals he believed in so strongly—including his belief that man should be celebrated for his contributions to his fellow man. That was the true legacy of Alfred Nobel.

Many years ago I, too, was left a legacy by a man whose ideals would come to touch the lives of people he would never know or even meet. I was a young police officer who believed more in the strength of my badge than in the heart that beat behind it. My world consisted of two distinct colors, shaded only by statutes and ordinances. I led the department in arrests and am probably still remembered for issuing a speeding ticket to a nun who believed that "sanctuary" applied when she drove onto the property of the convent with me in pursuit. I was only too happy to prove otherwise. I worked tirelessly in my solo attempt to stamp out all crime and transgression, and truly believed in my strategy of "zero tolerance."

Like any other workplace, a police department has a supervisory hierarchy that is guided by fate. By the luck of the draw you can be assigned to a sergeant or a boss who is competent or not; self-serving or nurturing; principled or unscrupulous. I was fortunate. My sergeant was not only highly respected, but respectful of others. I had seen him in action many times and truly admired his steely courage and quiet humor. I looked to him for guidance during the bloom of my young police career, and he did little to disappoint me.

But there was one conversation memorable above all others; 25 years later it still reverberates in my life like the tolling of a bell. Tom and I were having breakfast one chilly autumn morning, looking out of the greasy windows of an all-night diner as a fiery dawn broke over the desert. The discussion was fairly one-sided, with me recounting the long night's events, including a domestic dispute with a particularly argumentative husband whom I had gleefully handcuffed and jailed. When I was done bragging about my exploits, Tom said nothing for a moment. He simply looked at me over the streaked white porcelain coffee mug he held between his hands, and I knew by his silence that his thoughts were dancing.

Finally he placed the mug on its coffee-ringed saucer with a gentle clatter and said, "Randy, you're a good cop. You have all of the instincts necessary to sniff out bad guys, an excellent working knowledge of the law, and admirable dedication."

I basked in the remarks but felt uneasy about what else might be coming.

"But let me ask you one question," he went on.

Uh-oh, I thought.

"Can you tell me the difference between being a good cop . . . and a great cop?"

I must have stammered something, but to this day I cannot remember what. I do remember his eyes crinkling with amusement at my response, and then with the earnest expression that I came to know well in years to come.

"The difference between being a good cop and a great cop," he said, "is found in one word . . . compassion."

There are moments in your life that have special significance. Moments that create clarity in thought and perspective—and for me, that conversation was one. The concept of *compassion* came to define my view of not only my profession but also how I conduct my life. Most importantly, though, it is the message I have passed on to many a young and eager cop in whose future I am proud to have played a role. This is the rich legacy of thought that was bequeathed to me by a man who has proven again and again to be a mentor, friend and true hero.

I eventually left that police department for several reasons, the most significant being that I felt that the preferred leadership techniques of the agency's upper echelon were fear, intimidation and power. This led to poor morale amongst the employees that manifested itself as fragmented loyalties, promotions based on nepotism and personnel turnover. This continued for several years after I left until the then-chief retired . . . and a metamorphosis took place. The new chief brought with him an entirely different philosophy of leadership. He created an environment of unity by listening to the needs of his officers. Changes were made to how shift schedules were developed, on what promotions and assignments were based, and how discipline was meted out.

However, the most significant change was that the employees came to believe that their leaders cared about the law enforcement mission as well as about them. Recruitment and retention improved, officers distinguished themselves and were recognized for their achievements, and a culture of pride became evident.

Who was the man who ushered in this amazing change? You guessed it: the same man whose words and guidance had touched me those many years ago. Once again, Tom's philosophy trickled down through the men and women of the organization and would affect a new generation of young cops.

The decades have flown past, and just the other day I sat at my kitchen table with a mug of steaming coffee before me as I looked at two photographs displayed in the "shadowbox" commemorating my retirement from policing after 34 years. On one side was a black and white photo from my rookie days, and on the other a professional color portrait, complete with braid and gold bars. My thoughts drifted back through the moments that defined my career in a parade of joy, sadness, satisfaction and pride. As I gazed into the reflection in the glass that covered a box of memories, I caught a glimpse of two men in a diner on a morning when a single word changed one of them forever.

The Legacy of
CHARITY

*"If you haven't any charity in your heart, you have the worst
kind of heart trouble."*
— BOB HOPE

Charity is as much about what lies within one's heart
as it is about how one gives to others in need. Wealthy
people who donate millions to get a tax deduction,
or the celebrity/sports figure who has a need for
positive press relations and lends his or her name to an
organization that can capitalize on that name, definitely
do a service. But it is the passion that someone feels for
a cause that creates their LEGACY.

Experiencing the horrors of disease, poverty, or war
might scar the souls of some people, but can also create
a burning desire to help those who have experienced the
same pain. Or perhaps a person was forced to watch a
loved one face a terrible struggle, and that moved them
to dedicate their efforts to helping others. Either way,
those who leave the Legacy of Charity don't just open
their wallets...they open their hearts.

"If you get something and it's more than you expected,
you should always give some of it away."

BILL O'REILLY

Who is Bill O'Reilly? Bill O'Reilly currently serves as the host of FOX News Channel's (FNC) *The O'Reilly Factor* (weekdays 8PM/ET), the most-watched cable news show for the past 13 years. *The Factor*, as most people call it, is an unequaled blend of news analysis and hard-hitting investigative reporting that O'Reilly reminds us is the "No Spin Zone."

Bill graduated with a BA in history from Marist College and went on to earn his master's in broadcast journalism from Boston University and another master's degree in public administration from Harvard's Kennedy School of Government. He started his broadcasting career in Scranton, Pennsylvania, before moving on to report and anchor in other cities such as Dallas, Boston and New York. His national exposure began with CBS and ABC News, and as host of the first version of *Inside Edition*.

After writing five best-selling nonfiction books and his memoir, O'Reilly has been focusing on writing about history. *Killing Lincoln* was his first book in this genre, followed by *Killing Kennedy*, both sold millions and topped the *New York Times* bestseller list. *The History Channel* adapted both *Killing Lincoln* and *Killing Kennedy* into movies. The latter starred Rob Lowe in the title role and was given a high profile release in 2013 to coincide with the 50th anniversary of the assassination.

Meanwhile, after extensive research, O'Reilly also completed and released *Killing Jesus*, which reveals new details about Jesus's life and chronicles the events leading to his death. O'Reilly also writes a syndicated weekly newspaper column, along with making personal television appearances and *Keep It Pithy*, which is based on his love of language, and his frequent plea to those of you who write to him.

For more information please visit **www.billoreilly.com**.

•••

"Responsibility" is the watchword of a good journalist. You always have the opportunity to prove yourself. I think I did that when I covered the wars in El Salvador and Argentina. I had to prove myself, I had to do what it took to get the story even if it meant going into a zone that was really dangerous. I'm proud of the work I did then, because you never really know how you're going to react in those kinds of situations until you're in them.

But I don't think of myself in the capacity of being a hero. I have a personal code I adhere to strictly, in that if I say that I am going to do something, I am going to do it. So if I say I'd like to have lunch, we will have lunch; if I say that I will call you back, I will call you back, or my assistant will. I take what I say seriously so that I don't mislead anyone, ever.

That is my code: no misleading.

Professionally I've achieved a lot. I've been fortunate in my more than 35 years of journalism, and even before that with teaching high school. I always give my employer my best shot; I make sure I earn my salary and make money for other people. In our capitalistic system, that's what you do. I've always respected that process. I've never fluffed off or phoned it in; I've always earned my money, even when I was a younger man.

I'd say I've achieved what I have through perseverance and hard work more than talent. I was never the most talented guy on the block, and not the best student—but I worked very. Very hard.

I got my work ethic from my parents. They taught me that if I got knocked down, I should just get back up—and keep getting up because pretty soon you get knocked down again.

While I was growing up we didn't have a lot of money, but in our house it was always about other people rather than about *us*. There was no racism; there was a generosity of spirit that began with my mother. She was truly selfless. For example, other mothers in the neighborhood kind of rationed how they would drive kids to the movies or sporting events; they'd keep a tally and then say, "It's your turn." But my mother never did that; she just volunteered. My sister became a nurse, and I'm positive it's because of the example of my mother's selflessness. What I got from my mother was the idea that if you get something and it's more than you expected, you should always give some of it away. I've always done that—and it came from my mother.

When I was a kid, although I admired sports people like Willie Mays and Joe Namath, there wasn't really a particular person I knew

I wanted to be like. During my life I've looked around and observed how certain people accomplish things. If liked the way they did it, if they did it honestly, then I would adopt those behaviors. As I got older and met more people, I would sometimes think, *This is the kind of person I want to be*, but really it was an admiration of certain traits—like not hurting anyone through either words or actions, and not being misleading. I saw a lot of people get hurt when they were caught unaware by other people's deceit, and I said, "You know what? It isn't worth it!" To me, the short-term pain one feels from telling the truth in a difficult situation overrides the deceit, which is what really hurts the other person.

That's something Jesus espoused. I'm not a holy roller myself, even though I wrote about Jesus. I think spirituality is a personal deal—although I will say that my family history is Roman Catholic from the beginning of civilization, and I try to respect that tradition. Still, I'm not a guy who bases his life on spirituality—it's more of a mosaic for me.

Part of that mosaic is an emphasis on charity. We do a lot of children's charities, in particular: I think that a lot of children on this earth are being punished by stupid adults. Fathers who leave the home and mothers who are addicted to drugs or alcohol, poverty that is crushing and the parents can't figure their way out. The child isn't responsible for any of that, so we try to zero in on charities that work closely with children, and also military people who get hurt. I don't think that the VA is a very well-run organization, so we've stepped into that breach.

We try to act specifically, not generally. For example, we bought track chairs for guys who lost limbs or were blinded. The VA wasn't going to buy them, so we got 20 million dollars together to buy them ourselves.

I like charity to be directed toward things I've seen happen myself. I don't kick big money into big organizations; they already have enough and they have their machine pulling it in. I'm more of a niche person. For example, we give a lot of money to a San Diego organization called Responsibility, run by a man who's keeping Mexican children in Tijuana pretty much alive. He's a modern-day Dr. Tom Dooley, this guy. I did a story on him and saw the work he was doing down there, and for 25 years now we've been supporting him.

I'm not worried about my legacy. When I die I don't expect to get fair treatment by the press, but I think the people who have watched me for the last 18 years know who I am, and they'll remember me. Even after I retire they'll remember. Also, I've written my books and those will be there for the ages; they'll still be read long after I'm gone. That's a good legacy to have right there.

AUTHOR'S NOTE: It was the focus of our next story, Fr. Joe Carroll, who alerted us to the generosity of Bill O'Reilly. It seems O'Reilly has been supporting Father Joe's Villages for many years.

"If you can do more, you should do more."

FATHER JOE CARROLL

Who is **Father Joe Carroll?** When Father Joe Carroll became president of St. Vincent de Paul Center in 1982, the center was a small operation offering a daily lunch line and thrift store. But Father Joe had a larger vision in mind: an organization that could provide all the services a neighbor might need to transition from life on the streets to stable housing and independence. He called it a "one-stop shop" approach to rehabilitation.

In 1987, Father Joe realized his vision with the opening of the Joan Kroc Center, a transitional housing program that included a health clinic, job training, day program, dining hall and childcare—all under one roof. The innovative approach pioneered by Father Joe would eventually be replicated across the country as the "continuum of care" model of homeless service delivery.

Today, Father Joe's Villages is Southern California's largest residential homeless services provider. The multiagency organization prepares up to 4,000 meals and provides a continuum of care to more than 1,200 individuals every day. This includes over 200 children and over 200 military veterans. As an industry thought-leader, Father Joe's Villages offers innovative solutions to address the complex needs of the homeless, regardless of age, race, culture, or beliefs. The organization's primary goal is to transform lives and end the cycle of homelessness. To this end it provides food, clothing, housing, healthcare, education, job training, child development, and more. Father Joe's Villages has partner agencies in both San Diego and Riverside Counties.

In April of 2011, after nearly 30 years as president and CEO, and on the occasion of his 70th birthday, Father Joe Carroll transitioned to the title of President Emeritus. In his new role, Father Joe has stepped back from administrative duties to focus all his energies where he is most needed: fundraising for the Villages.

For more than three decades, Father Joe Carroll selflessly and tirelessly served the San Diego community. In that time he was the voice of, and advocate for, the homeless population throughout Southern California. Father Joe's contributions toward bettering the lives of our neighbors in need are truly immeasurable.

Father Joe's Villages is now and will always remain committed to carrying on this great legacy.

For more information please visit **www.my.neighbor.org**.

•••

My name is Father Joe Carroll and I was born and raised in the South Bronx, a tough part of New York. I was born on April 12, 1941, and came out to California when I was about 22. I always had bad arthritis and just didn't want another winter. This is my 50th anniversary living in California, but most people still think I'm a New Yorker, because I've never quite lost the accent.

In my family we had three brothers and four sisters—eight of us living in a two-bedroom apartment. By most of today's laws that would be child abuse. We were a typical Irish Catholic family. We partied on the weekends, and the church was across the street. That made it tough. If I wanted to cut out as a teenager, to skip Mass, my mom could see me by looking right out the window. We got a Catholic education—Catholic grade school, Catholic high school. So we were very much imbued with the neighborhood. I got involved with church youth groups. The church was our basketball center, our baseball center, our football team. We did everything through the church.

I thought it was a great life, a great young life! I became a Boy Scout at 11 and I'm still a member. Sixty years later, I'm still active in scouting. I couldn't give it up. Well known as a goody two-shoes in my youth, I could do no wrong. If you were to have a fight with me, the whole neighborhood would know it was your fault. Joey Caroll would never start a fight!

I was also a great Yankee fan, a fanatic Mickey Mantle fan. In fact, he was one of my first heroes. With all of his injuries, he always played. I have bad legs, too, and he taught me one of my great lessons in life: You never give up! You never use health as an excuse. Now I'm in a wheelchair, but I still go all the way downtown. Because he was one of my early heroes, I have baseballs signed by Mickey Mantle. I treasure them.

After joining the Boy Scouts, I played a little sports, managed a baseball team, coached for the kids. It was my way of giving back. Eventually, I moved out to California for the good weather. Then I joined the priesthood.

Ever since I was a kid, everyone said, "Joey Caroll is going to be a priest." But if there's anything people know about me, it's that I don't like being told what to do. So I resisted. I was going to be one of three things: a Boy Scout executive, a mathematician, or a priest. When I realized that the priest counts the collections, takes care of the math and can be a Boy Scout Chaplain, which I am, I was sold. I gave in and went to a seminary. For two years I attended and didn't tell the family. Upon hearing the news, my mother wrote me a note—"I always knew it would happen!" I didn't like that. . . .

I became a priest in '74. It was what they called "late vocation." Normally, priests are ordained at 25. I was ordained at 33. I went to seminary for four years, attended my first four years of college and was thrown out of school. I taught school for a year, then went back into seminary.

Before they kicked me out of college, they said I was the kind of priest who would sell gold-framed baptismal certificates. My attitude was, "If I make money, what's wrong with that?" They thought I was too entrepreneurial in my approach to priestly duties. They were right—and I still am. San Diego appreciates that. At the time, LA didn't. I parlayed my efforts into a way to raise funds! I enjoyed life, but have always been a wheeler and dealer. That's really how I got this job. The bishop asked who the biggest hustler, wheeler-dealer in San Diego was, and mine was the only name that made the list.

Since 1974 I've served in three different parishes. The first was Our Lady of Grace, which we nicknamed Our Lady of Money, because it was a really wealthy parish. Then I went to Saint Pius Chula Vista, which was more middle income. After that I went to Saint Rita's in south San Diego, which is ghetto. This included gang wars, shootings in the streets and the pastor carrying a gun. He was the only pastor I obeyed, possibly because he carried a .357 Magnum.

I could picture a kid breaking into a car in the parking lot. The pastor would come out and say, "What're you doing over there?" The kid would turn around with a screwdriver and say, "Back off, preacher!" And the pastor would pull out his .357 Magnum. Needless to say, they never messed around with the church.

Literally, I went from rich, to moderate, to poor, to homeless. I started helping the homeless in 1982, and, no, I didn't want the job! Bishop Leo T. Maher, who ended up being my boss for 20 years, got me involved. I argued with him. I said, "I really wanna be in the parish. I love parish work."

"Well," he said, "I have an opening in Needles, California."

Those were my choices: parish work in Needles, out in the Mojave Desert, or helping the homeless in San Diego.

When I got the job, I thought it would be a three- to five-year assignment and then I'd be back in the parish. I knew nothing about homelessness or shelters other than if you came to me, I'd send you downtown to whatever shelter there was. I was given the job at about the same time we bought some land the bishop wanted to build a shelter on. "Let's get a project for the homeless done," he said. "I know we have a priest committee that's supposed to approve all these projects—but you and me, that's it. We won't bring anybody else in on it. We need somebody who can find money and you're it!"

"What do you mean you're gonna build it without money in the bank?" people would say.

I'd just reply, "Oh, we're gonna raise the money as we build."

So I went around the country, from New York to Washington D.C., to learn about homeless shelters. I was embarrassed that we put people in such ramshackle buildings. The attitude back then was pretty much: if a building can't be used for anything else, let's offer it as a homeless shelter. Already you're saying something negative about the people you're helping. I made a commitment, then, that if I built a shelter, it would be first-class. I'm also a Republican. We like first class!

When I got involved, we had a thrift store located about a block away. But if you came in needing a new pair of shoes, I had to send you to Catholic Charities, which was 16 blocks away, to get a voucher. Then you had to walk back to the store for your free pair of shoes. But if you got the voucher, came back and we were closed, the voucher was no good. If you tried to use it the next day you couldn't.

I said, "Why don't we just give them the shoes?" The solution was so simple.

"If we build a shelter," I said, "it's got to be beautiful, because I've got to work there." Truth is, I like nice things. But it's also got to be comprehensive. It's got to have everything that you're going to need. All our shelters were patterned after my early ideas. They've got courtyards, water fountains, playgrounds—they're not your typical shelters. The same is true of all the buildings we constructed around here. The city built the new ballpark just to improve the neighborhood. The only good buildings in the neighborhood were our buildings.

The first shelter I built took five years to complete. I thought it would take three. It cost 10 to 12 million dollars. That did something to my brain. To me, a good way to raise money was to throw a spaghetti dinner and make 500 bucks. All of a sudden

I'm trying to figure out how to raise 12 million. It was like, you gotta be kidding me! I may be a good fundraiser; but there's a difference between a $500 spaghetti dinner and a multimillion dollar budget. How was I going to raise 12 million dollars?

The key was getting out and asking people. We actually rented a motel for my first shelter.

If you think back to the '80s, homelessness meant men, and some single women. In the early '80s, you didn't see families among the homeless. Now you see them, because the economy has changed. So our plans included a building for single men, and suddenly there were families. I said, "Whoa. We've got to change the design. We must find out what's going on."

Some shelters had created programs that didn't include job training. That's why I wanted everything in one complex, like hotels that have Italian restaurants and steak restaurants so guests don't have to go anywhere else. Once I'm in, I'm there.

It's all about rehab. If daily life is too frustrating, rehab isn't going to work—and with everything in one building, people can handle whatever has to be done. We ended up with 30 agencies in our facility in Las Vegas. We have full medical and dental. We do full and partial dentures on-site, as well as training, education, children's services, counselors. I mean, picture dealing with the homeless population. Some may be coming just for a meal, to see a doctor, or to go to counseling, because we have Alcoholics Anonymous, Narcotics Anonymous, and more counselors than you can name. On any given day, I have 12 psychiatrists across the street. That was the concept from the beginning: a "one-stop shopping" homeless shelter.

You can imagine the responsibilities. We house a thousand homeless people each night. Still, in 30 years I've had maybe four fights. Raise your voice anywhere on this property, and we have two German Shepherds to greet you. These are drug-sniffing dogs, so there are no drugs on these properties either. They're monitored every day. All of our apartments and houses are checked regularly. We call it tough love. I didn't build all this to have somebody mess it up. So we do what we can to enforce safety rules.

But the rewards are great. Of families, an average of 94 percent return to the workplace. For single adults, it's about 68 to 69 percent. We're dealing with real people here, so these percentages are huge.

I discovered was that when anyone prominent in the church came to San Diego to visit, my homeless shelter was Bishop Maher's showcase. He never said it to me, but this was what he was most proud of.

When he died, his brother, a monsignor in another diocese, gave speeches about how great Bishop Maher was. (When you're dead, you're great. When you're alive, you're a pain in the butt.) Afterward his brother called me up and said, "I don't understand it. They're all praising him for all these other things, when the thing he talked about most was your project."

Bishop Maher's legacy had two sides, a good one and a bad one. He was talked about, as he neared the end of his career, as "the last of the cowboys." That meant he took risks by giving a number of us great freedom. Other bishops would probably have just built one building and that would have been it: "We don't need any more. We've done our share." But Bishop Maher believed that if you can do more, you *should* do more. He taught me the true meaning of "share."

Another one of my heroes is a nun in Tijuana—Mother Antonia. Because she'd been divorced two or three times and was not allowed to be a regular nun in the Catholic church, Bishop Maher said, "Okay, sister, I'll make you an order of one."

At the time she lived in Beverly Hills. But at the Bishop's commission, she sold all her property and moved into the prison in Tijuana. That was where she wanted to be, and she was still there surrounded by murderers and rapists and drug dealers until her recent death. Those men still need to be loved, and she could do it. She convinced you of those men's worth.

Mother Antonia had a book written about her life. In the chapter where I appeared, I said, "She's the best thief I've ever met."

It was true! She'd go through one of our thrift stores loading up carloads of stuff that she said she was buying. Then she'd stop at the register and say, "Oh, I only brought three dollars with me." Of course we all fell in love with her.

Still, I had my moments. Once I saw her come in and I ran down from my office above the thrift store, and told her, "This is over with. You're not ripping me off anymore."

There she was, a little old lady of 70 or 80 years, who had heard my angry footsteps coming up behind her. Immediately, she turned around in her threadbare habit, dropped onto her knees and cried, "Padre, can I have your blessing?"

What was I supposed to do? I'm a Catholic priest and here's a nun on the floor, on her knees. Of course, I blessed her. Then they carried all this stuff out to her car.

Whenever I went to events she would hug me and say something like, "Thank you for the computers."

I would say, "What computers?"

My staff just couldn't say "No" to her. At this point, whenever they told me she had come by I would automatically ask, "What did it cost us?"

"Well, she took a truckload of this and a truckload of that . . ."

Thoughts of Mother Antonia's life's work always uplift me.

I have met many heroic people in my life. I learned from them. I emulated them. I tried to be a hero, too. I will be forever grateful for Bishop Maher, for Mother Antonia, even for Mickey Mantle. The best thing is that although these people did many great things, they didn't set out to impress anyone. They just wanted to be the best at what they were already—good people.

And maybe being your best, doing your best—even when nobody sees—is the most heroic choice of all.

The Legacy of
SHARING

"No one has ever become poor by giving."
— ANNE FRANK, *DIARY OF ANNE FRANK*

The concept of "sharing" is often impressed upon us when we are children. Our parents hopefully try to instill that quality in us in our formative years, even though it goes against the human nature of many. For most people, sharing is a learned behavior—and somehow, as we grow older, that particular aspect of our learning seems to diminish. Trite expressions like "I'm just looking out for number one!" and "Charity begins at home" serve as a collective reminder that we can easily rationalize certain aspects of our personalities.

Fortunately, most of us are capable of sharing in many different ways, and fairly frequently, as we journey through life. But when we witness those who go to extraordinary lengths to share of themselves by giving to others, we are often in awe. Some express their concern for their fellow man by sharing their monetary wealth; they might give great fortunes away. Others find that they can improve the lives of others by bringing their knowledge and experience to the classroom or community center.

Perhaps, though, those who share of themselves in ways great and small do so simply out of love—and isn't *sharing through love* the greatest legacy of all?

*"It is very important that we surround ourselves
with the greatest people in order to get the greatest results."*

GREG REID

Who is Greg Reid? Greg S. Reid is a natural entrepreneur known for his giving spirit and a knack for translating complicated situations into simple, digestible concepts.

As an action-taking phenomenon, strategy turns into results fast and furious, and relationships are deep and rich in the space he orbits.

Published in over 48 books, 28 best sellers, five motion pictures, and featured in countless magazines, Greg will share that the most valuable lessons we learn are also often the easiest ones to apply.

Recently, Greg has been hand selected by Frank Shankwitz (founder of the Make-A-Wish Foundation) to share Frank's true life story in a major motion picture entitled *Wish Man*.

For more information please visit **www.bookgreg.com**.

•••

When I look at the greatest moments of achievement in my life, I have to divide them into two categories. On the personal side, it was meeting the woman of my dreams and being given my first child, Colt Asher Reed. Fatherhood has been one of the greatest experiences I've ever had. Being a late-in-life dad, I never knew the pleasures of that type of *vibrancy*.

On the professional side, my greatest moment would have to be one that occurred after my first book was published and someone wrote to tell me they'd gotten some value from the book. That's tremendous, because when you first get into personal development you feel that if you can help just one person it would be worth it. I'm blessed to say that after almost 50 books in 35 different countries, I've had the opportunity to impact the lives of people all over the globe. That's got to be the greatest feeling one could ever have.

There's also the fact that I happen to be celebrating my 26th year of sobriety. I don't smoke or drink, I don't use drugs—and it's all a matter of choice.

There's a great serenity prayer that goes like this: "God, give me the serenity to accept the things I cannot change, the courage to change the things I can, and the wisdom to know the difference." That's a little mantra I not only speak every day, but live in my everyday life. It's been a great little tool to get me through the hardships that inevitably come down the road.

The greatest mentor I ever had was Charlie "Tremendous" Jones. He had a quote: "We are the same today as we will be in five years except for just two things: the people we meet and the books we read." Who you hang around with and what you put into your head will determine who you are.

So in high school, if you hung around the smoking section, you became a smoker; if you hung around the jocks you became a jock. If you hung around people who complain, gripe and moan, then that became the dialogue that played in your head. If you hung around people who were positive, uplifting and solution-searching, then that became the conversation.

It is very important that we surround ourselves with the greatest people in order to get the greatest results.

Charlie Jones is not only my hero; he's impacted the lives of millions of other people all across the globe. One of the things I loved about him was that for him it was always about honoring your mentors—and the way you honor them is by putting a spotlight on them and giving credit where credit is due. He never worried about being in the limelight himself, or being the front person. If he read a great book he'd tell everyone about it and put the spotlight on the writer's accomplishments. Charlie truly lived a life of service and abundance, and more importantly he understood the power of humility. For myself and for the millions of other people he touched, that was one of his greatest gifts. If you have to tell people you're rich, powerful and beautiful, chances are you're none of them!

Charlie was a motivational speaker and author, and probably one of the most beloved entertainers on stage in the personal development arena. Before he got cancer and lost his voice, he'd promised he would go on a world tour many years ahead. He didn't want to let anyone down so he decided to go even after he lost his voice. There he was, a motivational speaker who could not speak.

He called me up from Malaysia and said, "Greg, good news," he said so hoarsely I could barely understand him. "I completely lost my voice."

I said, "How is that good news, Charlie?"

"Because when I pick up the mic and whisper, people have to shut up and to hear me. I should have lost my voice years ago."

I think everything has a ripple effect. You know, one drop of water creates a ripple that goes out and spreads more ripples. For Charlie it was less about making a dollar and more about making an impact and more about leaving a message behind you, a wake of inspiration. What starts to happen is that you leave an example. You start living the life that others aspire to have. Rather than telling people what they should do, you do the things you think are great, and other people will aspire to do the same.

Charlie was a great mentor because he never once told me what I *wanted* to hear. He had a tough love mentality and gave opportunities to other people. He inspired me to do the same thing, so I carry on that legacy by putting the spotlight on other people.

"Use celebrities to make philanthropy cool."

MYRLIA PURCELL

Who is Myrlia Purcell? Myrlia Purcell wanted to create a website to publicize the many wonderful things that celebrities are doing to help the world, and to help charities by inspiring their celebrity supporters' fans to follow their heroes' example. The site, which now has a large team of dedicated contributing writers from four different continents, was launched in 2006 by husband-and-wife team, Steve & Myrlia Purcell, and conveys to its loyal viewers what the top stars are doing to make a positive difference in the world. Last year alone, the site had more than two million visitors and includes exclusive interviews and a database where fans can learn about their favorite stars' good deeds.

Myrlia is the owner of a small village ballet school, a writer of children's books and inspirational blogs, and the mother of two young children. She's also addicted to volunteer work. When not busy with any of the above, she likes to grow food in her garden and dreams of having enough land to keep her own fighting monks.

In 2013, she was voted as one of the Top 20 Women in Philanthropy by the Business of Giving, along with such women as Melinda Gates and Oprah Winfrey.

For more information please visit **www.looktothestars.org**.

•••

"Do you know what God wants me to tell you?" The smell of the man standing just inside the check-out area of the Kmart reached us well before we got close enough for him to talk to us about his message from God. His shaggy grey hair and ragged beard clearly had not been washed for some time, and his clothes might have had color once, but were so threadbare and filthy, my memories now are of flat, worn earth-tones.

He attempted to approach one shopper after another, each one rushing to get around him, carving a wide arc in the shiny tiled floor, offering him only haughtiness and uncomfortable, annoyed, indirect looks. Not one considered that, under different circumstances, they could have been there themselves.

I was only around three years old, so he paid me no attention as my mother led me across the hard, brightly lit space to run the man's holy gauntlet. He spoke to my mother, approaching with a look of conviction in his eyes. I could see that he wanted to make a difference to people somehow, and was oblivious to the effect he was actually having on his intended audience.

"Do you know what God wants me to tell you?" he asked my mother.

My mother met his gaze, looking him respectfully in the eye. "God spoke to me, too, and said I need to go now."

I remember a nod of recognition. My mother saw him as a human being, a soul, who deserved to be treated with respect, acknowledged despite his appearance and discomfiting behavior. I remember noticing his descent from agitated frustration into a place of peace; he exuded relief that someone else out there could see him. He wasn't invisible, he wasn't just a horrible apparition to be ignored and erased from both view and memory. He stepped aside and we continued on our way.

We reached the checkout aisle, and my mother told the woman behind the counter that there was a man who needed help just a short way back.

I remember the checker, a young woman, actually giggling. Why was she giggling? What was so funny about a lost man? She knew he was there. She thought he was funny, simply a crazy spectacle.

My mother suggested the shop call the police to get him some help, but the woman made it clear she wasn't going to do a thing to help him.

I looked up at my mother, who to me seemed like the only person in the world who had a heart, a soul, at that moment and in that place. "I want to be just like you when I grow up," I told her.

She smiled down at me, saying, "Thank you, but I hope you will be much better."

Still, I did want to be like her, able to offer love and respect to a stranger in need. And I wanted to be like the man, speaking out and offering messages of hope, continuing on, trying to help people indiscriminately, even when they cannot find it within themselves to say a kind word back.

Love, respect, and equality were always key attributes to share and develop in our family. My father always joked, in his "grumpy" voice, "I hate everybody equally."

My sister and I heard: "I'm a big softie who would do anything to help someone in need."

Perhaps we heard that only because that was what we saw, but it did make us laugh, and it made us think about how we should treat everyone. Not just everyone we knew, but *everyone*—the man in the car next to us at the traffic light, the lady walking her dog down the sidewalk, the old woman sitting on her porch as we drove past. Every one of them was someone for us to "hate equally."

Our father never had an unkind thing to say about anyone, but always had fun stories about their good points. He still always sees the best in people. (With the exception of the odd politician—but then, if you can't complain about politicians, what's the point of having them?)

During the recession of the '80s we saw my father turn down well-paying jobs because Ted, or Rob, or Frank was next in line for it, and needed the money to feed his family. He knew we could muddle through. They needed looking out for. Be strong, and look out for others—two things he demonstrated in the way he lived.

The seeds of compassion that were planted have stayed with me and blossomed as I've grown. I want to live in a world where people take the time to help each other, where we actually see the people we pass on the street. As fellow humans, we are here to share an experience together. We can offer each other smiles, respect and joy, or trouble and sorrow. It is our choice.

After the birth of my first daughter, I looked—really, deeply looked—at the world for the first time. What had until that moment been my playground was now suddenly a giant, horrifying, razor-wired, scalding hot, missile-launching, shark-infested ball of doom. It clearly needed child-proofing.

But what could I do to make a difference, while still being there for my baby? I could hardly start zooming from country to country on humanitarian missions to increase empathy levels around the globe. I was just one very tired, powerless person, living in a tiny London flat above a Chinese restaurant. My evenings were spent watching police helicopters fly past, shining searchlights in the windows, and my days often included a spell of yelling down at the would-be bike thieves who prowled the road while bike owners were grabbing a quick bite of lunch.

The momentum of all the crimes, greed and hatred seemed too much for me to fight against. I looked at my baby, now several months old, lying on her changing mat, and wondered how I could fix her world. Her legs and arms wiggled about clumsily, and she looked as helpless as I felt.

My thoughts travelled back some 27 years to the man in Kmart who tried so hard to tell people his message, and the harder he tried, the less they listened. How do you make the world listen?

I had an idea.

Several months earlier I had overheard two women who were looking over a magazine article about seven ways to make your life happier. Nothing on the list surprised them, until they came to:

"Do something nice for someone you've never met, who you will never see again."

The women hadn't the faintest idea how something like this could possibly help make them happier. They discussed it for a moment, decided the writer clearly didn't know what she was talking about, and moved on.

I nearly choked on my sandwich. How could they have never done something nice for a stranger? They were easily at least 20 years old—they had had plenty of time to do nice things!

Realizing that there would be nothing I could say to convince them (what does a strange, sandwich-eating eavesdropper know about anything?), I thought that if Madonna had walked into the room right at that moment and chatted with them about why she takes time to help others, those girls would have been out looking for strangers to help that afternoon.

So when my husband came home that evening, I told him my ambitious plan to make our baby's world a better place: use celebrities to make philanthropy cool.

I stood in our tiny living room, surrounded by soft toys, stained furniture and a giant diaper bin, trying to convince him that people were ready to make a positive change, and insisting that we should be the ones to lead it. We could help society turn away from tearing each other down, and encourage people to start building each other up. Instead of focusing on what people are doing wrong, we could start congratulating them for the good they do.

No one was doing it yet, despite gossip mags being ever-present. Clearly people wanted to know what celebrities were wearing and where they were going, so why not take that interest and tell the public what good the stars were doing?

We, ourselves, are not at all interested in celebrities, but we do appreciate how much they can influence the behavior of their fans. I wanted to show celebrity-watchers that people who have "everything" were actively seeking out opportunities to help others, traveling to remote, dusty, plumbing-deprived corners of the world to raise awareness and help make life better for strangers. They were spending their free time helping people they had never met, who they would never see again, and they couldn't get enough of it.

We had originally planned to make it a book project, with plans to send copies to schools for use in current events classes. We felt it would help put faces to events occurring around the world, as well as hopefully put geography into perspective.

We crafted a letter and sent it out to celebrities who we felt were positive and influential, asking them to answer four questions:

1. What do you feel is the biggest problem with the world today?
2. What steps would you take to correct this problem?
3. If you were to donate time or money to a charity, which charity would you choose?
4. What would you like to say to the world? This can be general thoughts, words of wisdom, a joke, or anything at all you would like to share.

The responses from the "gatekeepers"—the PR representatives and agents—were all very kind and supportive of the project; however, sadly, every one of them said their clients were simply too busy to participate.

Disheartened and disappointed, I was on the verge of giving up when a letter arrived from China. Of all the people on our list, there was just one who stood out from the rest as being a personal hero to me. While I respect what the others do, and love that they are doing it, only one person would have the power to make me go school-girl giggly, should I ever meet him. And he had answered my questions.

Not only had he answered the questions, but the letter stated that he thought it was a wonderful project, and requested that we send him a copy of the book when it was published.

Jackie Chan, my hero, had faith in our project. He had taken the time to answer the questions, and I couldn't just file it away and forget about it. If the gatekeepers wouldn't help me find out what their clients wanted to change about the world, I would just have to find it out myself.

And so, with the help of my captive software engineer—my loving, patient husband—*Look to the Stars* was born.

The two of us simply began, while our daughter slept at night, reading everything we could find about celebrities doing good things. We scanned the online gossip mags, we scoured charity websites, we checked fan sites and the then-popular MySpace pages. Sitting in the dark at our dining table, side-by-side, my husband would program the site to my specifications, and I would write down who was doing what. We created bio pages dedicated to the celebrities' philanthropic works, and linked them to non-profit pages on our site, allowing users to explore a variety of causes and celebrities in an entertaining, no-pressure environment.

It didn't take long before PR people started to notice us. They sent us news items, and invited us to cover their events. We found volunteers in the LA area, and sent them out to meet the celebrities, finding out in person what they wanted to say to their fans about making a difference. We ended up being invited to some events where no other media was permitted inside; people realized they could trust us to share an uplifting, gossip-free message.

Seven years on and still highly-trusted, we are now tracking and reporting on the philanthropic actions of thousands of celebrities around the world. Schoolchildren use our site, learning about world events and causes for their projects; nonprofits research our database to learn who might be willing to help direct attention to their work; and fans find out who is doing charity work in their area, learning how they can get involved.

We are often asked, "Why do they do it?"

Why do celebrities take the time to look into the eyes of someone they've never met and try to make those lives better?

Everyone has their own reasons. Some people might have personal experience that leads them to want to make a change, as is the case for many who take time to raise awareness about diseases. And yes, some of them might do it for publicity, which is a shame in some sense, but, in the larger scheme of things, everyone is winning in the end, with the nonprofit getting extra publicity in the process.

However, I believe many of them have experienced that special moment, the incredible, immeasurable feeling that you get when you acknowledge someone's worth, and brighten someone's life, for no reason other than because you have the power to do it.

JACQUELYN MITCHARD

Who is Jacquelyn Mitchard? Jacquelyn Mitchard is the #1 *New York Times* bestselling author of 20 books for adults, children, and young adults and the editor in chief of Merit Press, a realistic young adult imprint. A contributing editor for *More* magazine, she also is an instructor in the MFA in Writing program at Vermont College of Fine Arts. She lives on Cape Cod with her family.

For more information please visit **www.jacquelynmitchard.com**.

•••

I grew up in Chicago, the daughter to a plumber and a hardware store clerk. I was the first person on either side of my family to graduate high school—a big intercity high school with 4,000 students. Now, you try to live your life without regrets, but I've always been sorry I didn't take one of the available scholarships to Radcliff, or Smith College, or something like that. Still, my parents told me that being a blue-collar gal I would not be happy, so I ended up going to the University of Illinois at Champaign-Urbana.

While I was there, I met one of the greatest writing teachers of all time: Mark Castillo, who taught several better-known writers than me. So in the end, I lucked out.

After college I got a job as a waitress at a German restaurant. I had to wear a dirndl—picture *The Sound of Music*—you know, the lace-up thing? As a waitress you learn not to eat where you work because you see how everything is made, so one night I went out walking to get dinner, and I saw a sign that read "Reporters Wanted."

I thought, *I can do that*, although I hadn't done it one single day since high school. But I went into the office. It was dark. There was a guy sitting on a stool editing some copy. He was wearing bright green pants and a red and white striped shirt.

"Why are you dressed that way?" I asked.

He turned and looked me up and down. "Why are you dressed *that* way?"

I'd forgotten about my *Heidi* outfit.

That man became my first editor in the newspaper business—and, later, my first husband, who would die much too young.

I was also working on writing fiction. I sent a letter to an author named Ray Bradbury praising his short story "I Sing the Body Electric," which people know from the movie *The Electric Grandmother*. It's one of those stories, like *Charlotte's Web*, that you can't read without sobbing your head off. Ray sent me back a letter drawn all over in colored ink with vampires and dragons and witches and all kinds of creatures. All it said on the envelope was, "Jacquelyn Mitchard, A VERY GOOD WRITER INDEED, Madison, Wisconsin." And it got to me. The letter came to me in the newsroom, and I wrote back—which began a 35-year long conversation.

At the time Ray was 60 years old, a worldwide figure and a legend—the author of *Fahrenheit 451*, *The Martian Chronicles*, and things like that. To this day his books are on the curriculum of every 7th and 8th grade literature class in America. He was exceedingly kind to me and took up an enormous personal interest in me and gave me much of his time. When he was in the Madison area we had dinner together; I sent him my books and he commented on them. He was generous to me and many other writers. Even in the midst of writing some 20 novels and 600 short stories, having a family and traveling, lecturing and teaching, he took the time to write long, thoughtful letters to people he knew only as a few words on a page.

This was a great generosity of spirit from the kind of person who usually has someone to answer the phones and say, "I'm sorry; he isn't accepting any more engagements for the rest of the year."

To show how much influence Ray was, in 2012 a group of 26 writers including me, Joe Hill, Audrey Niffenegger, Alice Hoffman and Neil Gaiman published a collection of short stories called *Shadow Show: All New Stories in Celebration of Ray Bradbury*. Ray himself wrote the foreword shortly before he died. The book went on to win the Bram Stoker Award for best book of fantasy/horror that year, and some have called it the greatest collection of short stories ever written.

That was the kind of enthusiasm and loyalty Ray inspired. In 1996 it helped me sell my first novel, *The Deep End of the Ocean*.

Since then I've written another 20 books, including eight for young adults and four for children. *The Deep End of the Ocean* was the first selection Oprah Winfrey ever made for her book club. The funny thing is that no one thought that there would ever be a second book club episode on the show. The producers comforted me by saying, "Well, there will never be a second one but you'll always have been the first." Of course, there went on to be 57 Oprah's Book Club selections, all inspirational, and all bestsellers.

The Deep End of the Ocean was also made into a film. Actually many of my books have been optioned for film, and two were made, but there's only one you will ever see—*The Deep End of the Ocean*. It was a big movie and a very good movie in so many ways, and fun to see on the screen. In fact there has been nothing about my writing career that hasn't been fun, except maybe for writing about suffering, and my own self-doubt. I think that's why people start to drink: self-doubt. I just happened to suffer self-doubt without the drinking.

As my success grew I bought a house in Cape Cod and turned it into a retreat for women writers called One Writer's Place. I wanted to do something lasting. I wanted to make something real instead of just endowing a scholarship. Why only for women? Not because I don't like guys: I have five sons I love dearly. It was because . . . well, I thought women would be tidier. I thought they'd leave the house nicer—and after all, the retreat was for women coming from tough circumstances: divorce, death, a child who was sick or a parent who was older; things like that.

To get into One Writer's Place all you had to do was apply and prove that you hadn't just gotten out of prison for arson. You could come and stay for anything from a long weekend to two weeks. All the rooms were set up for writers, with desks and good lamps and comfortable beds, and there were four rooms named after writers I cared about from Massachusetts. During the three years the retreat ran, 30 writers came in and out, and three published books resulted. I also taught seminars there.

Then my second husband and I lost all our money in an investment scam. Most people are good, but the con man who did this was one of the worst people in the world. Chris and I had to put both our houses on the market. We figured the big, beautiful place in Wisconsin would never sell because it was set up for a gigantic family like our own. And we expected our tiny house in Massachusetts that used to be One Writer's Place not to sell because second homes weren't selling at the time.

It turned out that the big house sold in one minute and we had to be out of it the night before Thanksgiving. Now we live in the little house, and the kids sleep three to a room.

I'd had three sons in my first marriage. I wanted a girl, too, but after my first husband died I didn't think there would be a line of single guys out there saying, "You know what I want? I want a woman who's pushing 40 and has three grieving boys under the age of 12." So I adopted a little girl on my own.

Chris and I now have a mix of homemade and adopted children, nine altogether—and I never say which is which, except that the last two children we adopted were from Ethiopia.

Ironically, we adopted them the same week we lost all our money. At the time we did not intend to have any more children; Chris was even planning to go back to school so he could teach at the middle school level. Then we got a video from an acquaintance who was going to adopt two little girls from Ethiopia. In the video I saw two other beautiful little girls and asked who they were. I assumed they were the daughters of the social worker or something, because in the videos they conducted themselves like middle-class girls . . . which they had been—their dad was a sales analyst until he got AIDS.

My acquaintance said, "Those girls will never be adopted; the older one is almost twelve and the younger is five. No one is going to want them. In a few years the older one will have to leave the orphanage and support the little one, probably by becoming a prostitute."

And I thought, *Not that one.*

But the adoption was an immense struggle. For starters, it was difficult to bring into our lives children who had been orphaned by AIDS. Also, the older girl was bitter, and the younger girl frightened. They had never before met or even spoken to any white people, because Ethiopia was one African nation that was never colonized. Now here they were, part of this family of mostly Caucasian people.

To make matters worse, both Chris's family and mine deeply disapproved of the situation we were in. And I think Chris himself had some form of PTSD because we'd lost all our money at the same time; it was like he'd been gut shot or something. He was angry and defensive and shut off—all the things you would expect in a situation like that, but that are hard to bear when what you need is support and comfort.

But we couldn't pull back from the adoption. The mother had AIDS, the father had already died of AIDS. We weren't going to say "never mind." We were completely trashed financially, but did that mean we should trash our resumes as human beings as well?

I'm inspired by people who refuse to be less than fully engaged as human beings. Ray Bradbury was one of these; another is

Jane Goodall. Her work with chimpanzees helped prove that the medical community was doing hideous, torturous experiments on what were essentially nonhuman people; people who differed from us only in that their bodies were covered in fur and they didn't speak English.

She put a conscience in medical research regarding primates, but her legacy extends beyond that. Now people have to look in the mirror and see if perhaps, early in their careers, they too kept people in cages and did unspeakable things to them.

That's the kind of legacy I want to leave: the kind that exists in the present. It would be lovely to endow a room in a library, but to me it's more important to do things for and with people right now, because we aren't all guaranteed a tomorrow.

I tell people all the time that I'm not religious. One of my friends said, "No, you are, but they don't have your religion anymore. You're a Puritan. You get up every day and examine your soul and find out if you're doing the right thing and your soul is doing the right thing." She's right. Every day I try to be a nice person, but no one would ever *call* me a nice person because I'm far too crabby and exacting.

My daughter says, "Mom, you're brave and charming and you're gallant and generous but you're not nice." I'll take that; that's fine. That's how I hope to live every day until I close my eyes forever.

Through my writing I can change the world, I can make it better. My stories have an effect on people. Still, at the end of the day I want my headstone to read "Beloved Mother," not "She Never Missed a Deadline."

"We remember the moon race on TV, and those astronauts were our heroes—so I just try to give back what I can."

GREG OLSEN

Who is Greg Olsen? On October 1, 2005, Greg Olsen became the third private citizen to orbit the earth on the International Space Station. During his ten days in space he performed more than 150 orbits of the earth and logged almost 4 million miles of weightless travel.

Greg received his Ph.D. in materials science in 1971, after which he performed postdoctoral studies at the University of Port Elizabeth (South Africa), taught elementary physics classes, and worked as a research scientist at RCA Labs (Sarnoff Center). He's been awarded 12 patents, written more than 100 technical papers, co-authored several book chapters and given numerous invited lectures to both technical and trade journal audiences.

In 1984 he founded a fiber-optic detector manufacturer, which sold in 1990 for $12 million. He next founded Sensors Unlimited, a near-infrared camera manufacturer, which sold to Finisar Corp. for $600 million, was repurchased by the management team for $6 million, then sold again to Goodrich, Corp. in 2005 for $60 million.

Greg is active in many civic organizations including Trenton Big Brothers and Sisters, Trenton Boys and Girls Club, Trenton Soup Kitchen, Princeton Historical Society, Custer Battlefield Preservation Committee and Fairleigh Dickinson University and University of Virginia Alumni Associations.

He now performs numerous speaking engagements to encourage children—especially minorities and females—to consider careers in science and engineering.

For more information please visit **www.ghoventures.com**.

•••

Shortly after I returned from the space station I gave a presentation to kids in Bedford-Stuyvesant, a rough neighborhood in Brooklyn. Over 500 kids attended, and I expected them to throw tomatoes and stuff, but they were very quiet.

One guy who had looked me up on the Internet said, "Where did you get 20 million dollars to go to space?"

At the time I was a bit touchy about the money issue. People thought all I did was buy a ticket to the space station, like a tourist, which wasn't the case at all. There was a lot of training to go through, and while I was on the ISS I helped the crew conduct various life science experiments, and did several experiments of my own design. But I did have to pay, and this boy had asked where the money came from, so I said, "Well, I had a high-tech company."

He said, "What's a high-tech company?"

I started explaining the business, and he asked how I got to be a scientist. I said I studied math and science . . . and then it started clicking with me.

"Look," I said. "I got 20 million dollars to pay for a trip to the space station because I had this company I sold—but the reason I had the company in the first place was because I learned science and math. If you want a shot at something like what I did, *learn science and math*."

That was really the start of it. By now I've spoken to over 400 groups, especially high school students, on the importance of learning those subjects. I call my speech "From Entrepreneurship to Spaceship"—a joke on how I made my money and how I spent a big chunk of it. Of course I went into space for the thrill, just to be there, and I went for science. But after I got back I realized I also wanted to share my experience with other people.

I figured out I have a duty to *excite* kids. If I go to a school looking like Mr. Studious and give a formal lecture, nobody will listen. But I don't have a problem getting kids amped up. I put on my flight suit and play Joe Spaceman. I'm playing a role; I'm a vehicle for information. It's also a numbers thing. You might get kids excited when they're in the seventh grade, but as they get older . . . you just never know. I tend to avoid the upper-level high school classes because by then it's not cool to be excited.

I'm thrilled when I hear from one of those kids over the years that they've gone on to college for engineering.

In addition to urging kids to study math and science, I tell them how important it is to find mentors, especially when you're going into school. Finally a girl asked me, "Who's the most important mentor in *your* life?"

I'd never really thought about that. It's like, Well, this guy helped me with this, and this guy helped me get started . . . but then I thought, You know what? My most important mentor was my father, Sigurd.

Now, I wouldn't give my father very high marks as either a parent or a husband. He was a heavy drinker—I grew up thinking it was perfectly normal for a man to have three beers and a couple shots every day after work and then come home— and abusive, especially to my mom, who was also an alcoholic.

As for me and my sisters, you could call the way we were raised "neglect." My parents weren't that interested in what sports I played or what I did in college. When I was a kid one of my uncles would show up every year and say, "Hey, Greg, what do you mean you don't have a bat? Come on, let's go!" and we'd go get some baseball bats and he'd hit some grounders to me. My father never did stuff like that.

My dad had had a tough upbringing himself; he was an unhappy person. He and I didn't get along. We always clashed. In high school I was a big screw-up. I was convicted of juvenile delinquency in Bergen County. I flunked trigonometry my senior year. All I wanted to do was get out of school, buy a car, and pick up girls. My plan was to get into my father's electricians union. But since I was only 17 and still had a year of school to go, I figured I'd join the army first. This was pre-Vietnam; back then a guy joined the army so he could see the world. That was my goal: to join the army, and then the electricians union.

But I couldn't enlist in the military without my parents' permission. When I asked them to sign the paper, I waited for my father to say, "Why do you want to do some stupid f***in thing like that?" Then we'd get into an argument and I'd end up forging his signature and joining the army anyway. And that's what should have happened, based on past experience. But for reasons unknown, my father was reasonable that day. He said, "Look, Greg, it's getting hard to get into the union, and they require you to have six months of college. So why don't you try that, and if you don't like it, I'll sign the paper."

Now, I could run my father down about how he didn't come to my Little League games and football games and all that kind of stuff, but right then, at the most important moment of my life, he was there for me. I ended up going to college despite my poor performance in high school, and of course college turned my whole life around. Instead of an electrician's license, I ended up with a Ph.D. in materials science. That led to me forming my first company, which led, eventually, to my being able to travel into space.

Another thing is that I learned a lot by watching my father. Not from him formally teaching me, because he was very narrow-minded and a hard-ass. But he was very good at what he did, so I didn't ask him to show me things, I just watched him.

And what I learned stuck with me. For example, a while ago my garage door broke. I could have called Sears and had them come fix it, but thanks to my father, I'm handy. He instilled it in my head to never *ever* call a repairman, no matter what broke. He'd just figure out anything, so I have that left in me.

I always felt like I had to figure life out because no one else was going to figure it out for me. For a long time I thought kids were lucky when they had parents who taught them about life—but now, looking back, I think I was luckier than these poor kids who have golden chains put on them. My grandson is 12 years old and my daughter won't even allow him to go into Central Park, even though it's a really safe place these days.

Kids today also don't have the motivational things that I had growing up: Sputnik; Kennedy's speech about putting a man on the moon by the end of the 1960s; things like that. You don't hear about space much at all anymore. We remember the moon race on TV, and those astronauts were our heroes—so I just try to give back what I can.

It's not just public speaking. Back when I was in college, I worked in the New York City electrician's union, IBEW Local 3, for four years. They called us "summer helpers" and gave us fourth-year apprentice pay; you can imagine how much that was. Shortly after the 9/11 terrorist attacks I started giving out four-year general scholarships through the union. There were 20 union members in the World Trade Center that day, and we lost 17 of them. I didn't know any of the victims personally, but there's a sense of brotherhood.

By now I've given out more than fifty scholarships to colleges all across the country. It's heartwarming when I get a letter saying, "I got a job at a utility doing this."

The scholarships are given in my father's name. He died 36 years ago, slumped over the table with a Camel in his hand. The only thing missing was his beer. Every now and then at the breakfasts we have where we give out scholarships, some old geezer will come up to me and tell me he remembers my old man. He'll say, "Didn't they used to call him Siggy?"

When it comes to giving back and inspiring others, I think the drive to do it is an innate thing. Once I was speaking to a class of Chinese MBA students. As a rule, Chinese students are quiet and don't ask you certain questions because they don't want to embarrass you, but this one class asked me about religion, which surprised me. In fact they really hectored me: Did I find God up in the spaceship?

The truth is, I'm not religious. My wife was Jewish, and I grew up Lutheran, but as soon as my church education was over, that was the last I saw of it. My wife and I didn't bring our daughters up around religion, but they certainly know right from wrong. I think most people naturally want to help others, but people often feel they can't. That's not true. Just because someone has money doesn't mean they're helping others more than someone else.

In addition to my talks at schools, I enjoy speaking before adult groups on the subject of not giving up on yourself and your dreams and goals. I was 60 years old when I went up in space. I've been very fortunate, of course, but when I was 54 my net worth was zero. My message is: "Don't give up on yourself." You might be flunking trigonometry, and there are three guys above you with straight As, but don't assume it's easy for them because it's not. Just don't give up on *yourself*.

I believe when you can complete a task, that gives you some value. Whether it's kids, adults, no matter who you are, it doesn't matter—the secret is: *Don't give up*.

*"This led to leadership development expeditions to places
like Mt. Everest Base Camp, the Inca Trails,
and the top of Mt. Kilimanjaro."*

WERNER BERGER

Who is Werner Berger? Werner Berger is a corporate consultant in the domain of leadership and inspired selling, and the oldest person in the world to have climbed the Seven Summits, the highest mountains on each of the seven continents; which, of course, includes Mt. Everest.

For more information please visit **www.BackFromTheEdge Movie.com**.

•••

In September 1994 I met the famous author and workshop leader Robert G. Allen—a chance encounter that changed my life. We talked about personal development, and although I'd run a successful business for years and thought I knew it all, he opened my eyes to much greater possibilities in thinking, being, and the creation of wealth. At the time he was also advocating the use of nutritional supplements, since our foods were so nutritionally depleted.

"I don't need them," I said. "I eat right."

Wrong.

The more I looked into this issue, the more convinced I became that we were dealing with a potential health crisis in the making. My research showed that our foods were indeed nutritionally depleted. Most fast and processed foods did nothing for our health; in fact they were mostly detrimental. And of the thousands of supplements on the market, only a few had any real value to the human body. Ever since then I've taken the best supplements I can find. I'm healthier and have more energy, and am clear that without the supplements I would not have the vitality and endurance to still be climbing mountains at what some would consider an advanced age.

But that is not where Bob Allen's influence on my life ends. A few years ago we were talking about my climbing, and my quest as a corporate consultant to change the landscape of leadership. Most corporate employees do not like their jobs, which usually equates to not liking their "boss." The main reason for this is the boss's lack of leadership skills.

"Combine your climbing and leadership coaching with transformational, adventure travel experiences for senior executives," was Mr. Allen's advice. This led to leadership development expeditions to places like Mt. Everest Base Camp, the Inca Trails, and the top of Mt. Kilimanjaro—all life-changing experiences and much fun.

A final salute to Mr. Allen—I met my wife, Heshie, at one of his boot camps!

Very early in my relationship with Heshie we concluded that we were soul mates. However, in many ways our orientations to life seemed diametrically opposed. We came together from different cultures and different continents. Her life coach, Laura Szabo Cohen, called our relationship "God's joke," and encouraged each of us to look deep inside to see what made us tick and what triggered the attraction.

These interchanges, plus Laura's coaching, launched a path of self-discovery that had been hidden from me by my perception of who I thought I *should* be in the world. I had to face the fact that although I knew a lot about human "being-ness," I didn't know much about how to naturally "be" in my own life. As with you, I'm still a work in progress and, thankfully, got a boost into this rewarding and fulfilling journey by coaches and great mentors. "When I grow up I will . . . oh yes, climb high in life."

"Today was your lucky day.
You got to meet a real hero."

JOHN L. SMITH

Who **is John L. Smith?** John L. Smith is a prize-winning journalist whose column in the *Las Vegas Review-Journal* is the most widely-read newspaper feature in Nevada. In addition, John is the author of many books, including *Of Rats and Men: Oscar Goodman's Life from Mob Mouthpiece to Mayor of Las Vegas; No Limit: The Rise and Fall of Bob Stupak; The Animal in Hollywood* with Anthony Fiato; *Running Scared: The Life and Treacherous Times of Las Vegas Casino King Steve Wynn; Sharks in the Desert: The Founding Fathers and Current Kings of Las Vegas;* and most recently, *Bluegrass Days, Neon Nights: High Rolling with Happy Chandler's Wayward Son, Dan Chandler.*

John lives in Las Vegas and carries the distinction of being a fourth-generation Nevadan.

For more information please visit **www.ameliaslongjourney. com.**

•••

As a boy growing up in the 1960s in Southern Nevada, I found my heroes shifting with the sports seasons.

As spring turned and faded into summer, Sandy Koufax was king. I was fiercely loyal to the lanky left-hander and followed every game he pitched on radio, black-and-white television, and in the sports pages. He never seemed to lose in those days.

Come fall, the Green Bay Packers took the field. And that meant idolizing No. 15, Bart Starr. I sent away for a Packers pennant and pinned it to the wall of my bedroom. By winter, it was NBA center Lew Alcindor, later known Kareem Abdul-Jabbar, who would come sky-hooking into my imagination. And when spring rolled around again, Koufax held my imagination and respect. Sandy, most of all, epitomized my ideal of grace under pressure.

But it was only after I met Amelia Rose that I truly began to understand the meaning of courage and heroism.

She wasn't a sport page superstar, and didn't have a single league record to her name. Amelia was a little pink bundle of pure goodness I first met on March 15, 1996.

As all children should, she changed her proud parents' lives forever. There's nothing like a newborn to make you reassess your priorities, and so it was with Amelia. My wife and I couldn't believe our great fortune that we would be blessed with an adorable girl with curly golden hair, the kind that made strangers approach us and comment on its beauty.

For several years we figured we had this parenting game licked. Amelia was ahead of every curve in elementary school and was a wellspring of joy in our hearts.

She occasionally complained of headaches and morning nausea, and we responded with trips to the pediatrician, but her complaints were attributed to the usual childhood maladies of sour stomach, schooltime nerves, or the latest flu virus that kids passed back and forth like a hot potato.

It was only when the headaches became acute that a physician moved for an MRI, which easily discovered the walnut-sized tumor in the middle of her brain. Our precocious eight-year-old had hours to live, and we reacted by having her immediately transported to St. Joseph's Hospital and Barrow Neurological in Phoenix. Dr. Kris Smith—no relation, although I'll celebrate his name the rest of my life—reassured us in the waiting room by saying: "Your daughter will get through this surgery. It's every day after this that will be the challenge."

We could not know then how prophetic his words would be.

Amelia pulled through the surgery with flying colors. She lost some of her beautiful hair and had an eight-inch scar across her scalp from the massive operation. But just hours after regaining consciousness she appeared to be returning to her sweet self.

But the tumor was malignant, a mixed-cell germinoma, and she would need to receive chemotherapy and radiation. In the fall of 2004, we embarked on that chapter of her recovery and spent the next seven months helping her through the ordeal. Family and friends gathered around us, and in many ways we were blessed by abundance even as the medical bills sapped our insurance and drained our savings account.

None of that mattered, of course, for at the end of that tunnel Amelia's doctors said all the signs were good and she was headed toward a full recovery. We returned to Southern Nevada in April 2005 and resumed our lives.

When she complained of back pain a few weeks later we hoped it was strain from playing so much with her friends, but there was no taking chances. She was immediately given an

MRI, which showed that the cancer had relapsed in her upper spine. We hadn't finished unpacking all our boxes from the previous medical sojourn.

This time, our physicians said, the issue was even more dire. The cancer had managed to survive the substantial chemotherapy she'd been given, and that left only one alternative: a high-dose chemotherapy and what they called a stem-cell rescue. Because the cancer hadn't spread to her blood, she was able to have her own stem cells harvested. We chose Children's Hospital Los Angeles for the treatment.

And the second chapter began, this time on the edge of Hollywood in a crowded Ronald McDonald House located just around the corner from the hospital, whose oncology floor was bursting with patients from throughout the hemisphere. This time, Amelia would not only lose her energy and her hair, but because of the severity of the chemo drugs she'd also lose her skin, toenails. Even her tongue would peel during the excruciating procedure that would bring her to the brink of death and, if all went according to plan, return her to us following a stem-cell infusion cancer-free.

When she could receive visitors, the hospital sometimes brought in professional athletes to greet and sign autographs for the children. As a lifelong baseball fan, Amelia was excited to meet three members of the Los Angeles Dodgers, including one player who'd gained a notorious reputation as a malcontent and prima donna.

After the brief meet-and-greet, in the hallway I thanked the ballplayers for stopping by and said to the multimillionaire superstar, "Today was your lucky day. You got to meet a real hero."

He looked confused and declined to answer.

In the weeks that followed, Amelia struggled but somehow she made it through. The nerve damage caused by the cancer treatment took away her ability to walk. She lost some feeling in her fingers, some of her hearing, and following the heavy brain and spine radiation a percentage of her cognition. But she did not lose her ability to smile, to laugh and tell jokes, perform card tricks and, when her energy permitted, attend school with her friends.

All she had to do was endure daily neuropathic leg pain that would drive the strong to the brink of insanity. To get to school she had to learn to use a wheelchair, work through countless hours of physical and occupational therapy, watch children and adults avert their eyes from her as we pushed through local shopping malls, and suffer the arrows of friends whose young lives moved too quickly for a girl in a wheelchair.

Along the way, we enjoyed watching our local minor-league baseball team play. Amelia was honored before a Seattle Mariners/Chicago Cubs spring training game and threw out the first pitch. (For the record, it was a strike.) When traveling, usually to a doctor's visit, we would catch a big-league game as a special treat. But I had long since lost my interest in the sports page and its celebrities. I had my own hero at home showing grace under pressure every day.

A few more years passed, and our marriage fell apart. Amelia accepted the changes. She continued to struggle to succeed, and her adoring parents never forgot that the most important thing that would ever happen in their lives was still blessing them every day.

Amelia kept moving, gaining more energy and remaining cancer free, but also suffering from all the after-effects of the cancer, surgery, chemotherapy and radiation. We joined the local childhood cancer research fund-raising effort at McMullan's Irish Pub that's associated with the St. Baldrick's Foundation, and for seven springs running Amelia shaved her dad's head. Our ever-growing group at the pub and across the valley managed to raise well over $1 million in just a few years.

Classroom studies that had been a breeze grew increasingly difficult, but Amelia plugged away with few complaints. She went to therapy twice a week, stretched at home and kept working to get any improvement from her nerve-damaged legs. As the agonizing electrical shocks associated with the neuropathy gradually subsided, she stayed away from the prescription painkillers and worked at getting stronger.

Today, Amelia deals not only with her physical challenges, but with hormonal ones as well. The fallout from her medical ordeal continues, and she takes a variety of medications and hormone supplements. She continues her physical therapy, too. Her arduous journey should remind all of us that the future of cancer treatment in America is not just about finding cures and improving therapies, but designing a program in which after-care receives as much detailed attention as that first surgery itself. Dr. Smith had been right all those years ago when he said my daughter would survive her brain operation, but that every day that would follow would be the challenge.

Childhood cancer research in this great nation receives just four percent of the funding set aside by the federal government—four percent! And yet it's also true that stricken children, heroes every one, are often more resilient patients than their adult counterparts. They fight because they believe, because their hearts are pure and their trust is unconditional.

Increased government funding for research is the least we can do for our children. Striving for a greater understanding of the importance of after-care to the quality of life of the patients and their families is an essential part of the picture.

My daughter is a hero not because she was a kid with cancer who survived, but because she carries on with remarkable grace despite the ravages of the disease and treatment.

While she lives her life and plays the cards she's been dealt, she reminds her old man and countless others what a true hero looks like. She's right in my own home. Her name is Amelia.

The Legacy of
LEADERSHIP

*"Leadership is the art of getting someone else to do something
you want done because he wants to do it."*
— Dwight D. Eisenhower

Leadership might be the most intangible of all human traits. Ask ten people what it is and you will receive ten different answers. At the risk of being irreverent, I'm reminded of the time the Supreme Court of the United States struggled with a landmark case that involved defining pornography, and Justice Potter Stewart stated that he might not be able to define it but "I know it when I see it." The same can be said of leadership.

A true leader invokes loyalty—in and of itself a feat worthy of respect. But those who possess the greatest qualities of leadership bring loyalty to an entirely different level; those they lead are willing to quite literally entrust their lives and future to that person.

There is no greater privilege than to lead others, nor a greater responsibility, and that is the true Legacy of Leadership.

"We'd gather a small, elite group of men and women and just go out and provide good care and education with no strings attached."

ERIC LINDER

W**ho is Eric Linder?** At the age of 16, Eric Linder discovered that he enjoyed the excitement of providing emergency medicine. While still a senior in high school, he became a licensed Emergency Medical Technician, and at 17 he joined the US Air Force's Crash, Fire & Rescue team. Later, as an air force officer, he was decorated for service in Operations Desert Shield and Desert Storm.

While working in Nevada at the Desert Warfare Training School he went on a ride-along with a Las Vegas police officer. Shortly after that he entered the police academy. As an officer for Las Vegas Metro he worked assignments ranging from patrol to gangs to felon apprehension. Then he took a three year leave of absence to go to Israel and serve in the special forces sections of the police and military.

He returned to Las Vegas with a whole new skill set.

After 9/11 he joined the newly redesigned Federal Air Marshal Program, then moved on to become director of major crime for the United Nations peacekeeping mission in Kosovo. He was granted the UN medal for his work there.

While working as director of health, safety and security for a well-known Fortune 500 company, he returned to school in order to bridge his medical licenses from Israel to America. He earned his license as a remote medical practitioner, which involved traveling to the jungles of Belize to provide healthcare to indigenous peoples in remote locations. Later, he made not one but two similar journeys into Uganda.

In 2011, Eric and some friends came up with a powerful idea: put together a team comprised of individuals with backgrounds as either special forces medical personnel or ultra-athletes, and send them out to provide healthcare and education in the most remote and difficult regions of the world. After a few deployments to the jungles of Belize and Guatemala, the team decided the best working number for such a group was five: few enough to get funding, too few for cliques to form, but the right number to ensure there would always be a winning vote.

That was how Team 5 Foundation was born. The concept was for five medical personnel to deploy to a remote location, teach the locals a two-day class in advanced Western medicine, run five mobile clinics in five days, and then leave—after donating enough medical supplies to sustain the location for six months, of course.

To date, Team 5 has completed ten such deployments in four different countries; taught more than 125 healthcare workers in midwifery, emergency care and primary care; treated over 6,000 patients; conducted more than 1,000 ultrasounds; and helped to disseminate over two million dollars in supplies.

Eric's vision is to build Team 5 to the point where it can run at least three missions per year in locations of the world that are usually overlooked. A nonprofit organization, Team 5 has no religious or political involvement.

They're there for only one reason: to do the right thing.

For more information please visit **www.team-5.org**.

•••

I grew up with one brother and two sisters in New Jersey. I was a very active kid—in fact I had ADD, but stuff like that wasn't recognized back then, so I was just one of those kids who bounced off the walls and had to repeat classes a lot. My father was a traveling salesman and my mom a stay-at-home mother. But she'd been a teacher, so she knew I had problems. She had me work with tutors to find out exactly what was wrong.

I was a gymnast, so my mother hired a tutor who was also a gymnast. I'd go to the gym and do things that would correlate with math. Then they found out I was dyslexic, so the tutor helped me with that, too. They put numbers down on the trampoline so instead of just sitting there bored, I'd do a flip from one number to the next. I would be adding and subtracting or dividing to keep me mentally active, and I'd learn these things quickly.

Next came the deafness. I remember walking down a road with my mom yelling and yelling, and I couldn't hear anything. She grabbed me and turned me around and said, "Did you hear me?"

And I said, "No."

Next thing you know, my mother was taking me to the doctor; I ended up having tubes in my ears for about six months.

My dad did pretty well financially, so to keep me active as a kid they put me through adventure camps. Sports didn't really do anything for me, so I'd go kayaking down the Delaware River and spend weeks camping out, learning how to rappel and doing all the other things that led me to where I'm at today.

I also went to travel camps. I'd climb on a Greyhound bus and be gone for 30 days, riding from New Jersey to California and back. At night we'd pitch a tent, and during the day we'd be riding horses, boating, kayaking and all sorts of wilderness stuff.

When I was 16, a friend talked me into being a volunteer on a rescue squad in Jamesburg, New Jersey. I said sure—and my first day on the squad I was called to a site where a kid had fallen through a window and sliced both his wrists open. So here I am—a kid myself, with no training, and friend who'd just finished his training, and there's nobody else available because the squad is part-time volunteer work.

We were bandaging this guy up when other squad members finally showed up and were all shocked and impressed with what we'd done, and suggested I volunteer there. So by the age of 18, I was already an EMT, which was a new concept back in the 1980s.

After I graduated from the New Jersey State Police Rescue School and became a member, I decided to join the military—which was a big no-no in my family because my dad had been drafted during the Vietnam War period. Everyone kept saying it's dangerous and not to do it, but I told them it was what I really want to do. I really wanted to be a marine, but being 17 years old and needing my parents signature, the air force was the only option I had.

So I joined the air force and did rescue work and became a paramedic while attending college in the UK where I was stationed. I enjoyed it, but I knew there was more I could do. I knew I wanted to get into law enforcement later, so I cross-trained with the Air Force Security Police while I was transitioning from active duty into the Reserves. I was an honor graduate, and got stationed in the reserves at McGuire Air Force Base.

While I was there I went to the East Brunswick Police Department where I'd been an explorer as a kid. I asked if there were any openings. They said no, except as a part-time cop, or what they called "specials." They knew who I was and what my history and qualifications were, and told me they'd send me to the Monmouth Police Academy.

While I was in the academy I got called into reserve duty for the war—I was assigned to protect dignitaries when Desert Shield/ Storm was active. As a reservist I worked from McGuire AFB first, and was later sent to Nellis AFB. They dumped me off at Silver Flag Alpha, which is up near Indian Springs in Nevada, to be "OPFOR"—"Opposing Force," the bad guys in Desert Warfare Training Center.

I had a blast doing that. On weekends we'd come to town in Las Vegas, where I happened to meet Jodi Vanek, a detective assigned to Metro Gang Unit while he was working the streets downtown. After chatting and finding out I was a cop in Jersey, he asked if I wanted to do a ride-along, and I said yes. I went with him one night chasing bad guys, and he had me fill out an "interest card." But I really never thought much about it.

I returned to my reserve post, and a month later was back in New Jersey because the war had ended and I'd finished the police academy. A few weeks later a letter arrived from Las Vegas Metro asking if I wanted to go out and test for the police department. Tired of the snow, I jumped on the opportunity.

And that's how I ended up a police officer in Vegas.

I was on Metro for 12 years, ten of them in Vegas itself and two in Israel on a civil service fellowship to learn counter-terrorism and tactical medicine. To this day I'm the only person to have ever been picked for that.

In Israel I was supposed to be working with the police on tactical medicine, but after I'd been there for two weeks they said, "You're Jewish, you need to do military service time. You only have to do six months and then you'll be in the reserves."

Because I was initially recruited to be assigned to the police counter-terror units, I asked if I could test for a special forces unit of the Israel Defense Forces. Without hesitation, they said, "Yes." I tested out for the pararescue unit in the Israeli Air Force, and made it.

I ended up becoming a PJ, a parajumper as it was called at the time, in the combat search and rescue unit in Israel. This unit was designed to respond when people got stuck behind enemy lines and cried for help. We were basically a Blackhawk unit: four to six warriors per helicopter. Everybody has a designated job, and mine was the special forces medic. I would do surgical procedures, emergency medicine for wounds inflicted by IEDs and bullets, and anything else that might present itself. There was also a surgeon, but he never left the helicopter because he wasn't tactically trained; he was there to assist the wounded I brought to him. We'd do whatever procures were necessary until we got the wounded person to the hospital and into the operating room.

I was a PJ for two years, and also did training for the IAF pilots in SERE, the police force, and worked with the Yasam, the counter-terror unit for Israel in the northern district. I was in the Lebanon War, multiple missions in and out, then did ten years in the Israeli Reserves, returning for three weeks out of every year to do my service. I retired as a sergeant major, the highest non-commissioned rank in the military.

After my two years in Israel I came back to Las Vegas Metro as a police officer and to teach counter-terrorism. I worked in fugitive detail and gang unit intel and was a part-time negotiator. When 9/11 hit, they used me to teach the ATF and FBI in Las Vegas for profiling Middle Eastern terrorists and suicide bombers.

Then the federal government came and asked me to help kick off the air marshals. They offered me a very large salary—double what I was making at Metro—but I mostly saw it as a chance to do something different. Plus there was some bad feelings there on Metro, some promises that had been made to me when I went to Israel that had not been kept, so I left to pursue a new career in counter-terror.

In the air marshalls I was the lead medic and the instructor for profiling & Middle Eastern affairs. I created a course to teach cultural differences in the Middle Eastern world, which is still used today in FLETC, the Federal Law Enforcement Training Center.

But I never lost my interest in the medical field, and especially the kind of care that takes place outside the average hospital. When I returned from Israel I began to transition my licenses to their equivalents in the US. A company called GORGRP works with the University of Nebraska Medical Center and other schools to try and bridge the gap of international medical professionals to find a way to bring more people here with specialized skills. With my PJ license in Israel, I began earning the licensing equivalent to the level of a PA, a physician's assistant.

I also did a one-year certification course called Remote Medical Practitioner, which is based on the military's Advanced

Tactical Practitioners course, with clinical medicine added to the curriculum. We were kind of like the MacGyvers of medicine, dealing with everything from dental emergencies to altitude sickness to wilderness medicine to hypothermia—any kind of medicine you could think of that might occur in austere conditions. I cross-trained with this course for a year, then took another advanced class from RMI called Remote Medicine for the Advanced Provider and became an instructor in aviation medicine. For my residency I had to be in a Third World country and on my own for thirty days. I went to Belize in Central America and basically just walked into the jungle. I did medicine from village to village, and ended up in the operating room assisting surgeries at the Belmopan Hospital at the capital.

Then, in 2009, I started my fellowship in Austere Medicine and Wilderness Medicine at the Fellow Academy Wilderness Medicine with the Wilderness Medical Society. That basically means you become an expert in travel and wilderness medicine, learning how to deal with all the different species of insects and venomous reptiles and sea creatures, dealing in high altitudes, low depths and survival tactics including the use of primitive tools. It's a very hard fellowship to get because you don't just sit behind a desk; you have to actually go out and pass the courses in extreme conditions and then come back and get your work reviewed by the society board members. It took me three years to earn the necessary credits and be honored as a fellow.

While I was in Belize I realized I liked helping out in these developing countries where most of the people had absolutely nothing, not even clothing. One day one of my professors from UNMC called and said they were going to be the first mission to Gulu, Uganda. He said I was exactly the person they needed on the team because the doctors and nurses they already had were used to working in hospitals, not in the elements and in a displacement camp. They were specialists. One doctor did pediatrics; another plastic surgery; one was a cardiologist, and so forth—very skilled practitioners, but they were used to working in a sterile environment, a hospital.

I was different. Someone with my background and qualifications could be dropped at any location and say, "Oh, I can do that." I had to be willing and able to do anything from dental care to delivering babies and performing minor surgeries without any help.

So we went to Northern Uganda, a trip that took over 24 hours from the USA and another hour and a half from Gulu. We were in a displacement camp where people lived in mud huts and had to walk three hours a day to get a jug of water that they carried back on their head. You would see the mother with a large plastic jug, her teen with a smaller one and a five-year-old practicing with hers. It was heartbreaking but at the same time reminded us how good we have things at home, where we use just enough energy to turn a knob to get clean water.

We went there with a small group of people, the first whites the villagers had ever seen; the children kept touching my skin and beard, as they were different than their own. The first day a hundred people came by. The next day the line was over a mile long, no kidding. As we drove up the dirt road that served as the only lane for both directions of traffic, we saw the line of indigenous locals walking with water and food because they knew it would be a long wait before they saw care.

It went on like that every day for a week. We made only a small dent. I decided there needed to be more people out there doing this kind of work, but I was told no one was willing to do it because no one stays out after dark, it was way too dangerous. This was the area where the LRA, the Lord's Resistance Army, had forced the people of northern Uganda to leave their villages and enter government-run camps for internally displaced persons (IDPs). These camps were supposedly created for the safety of the people, but were rife with disease and violence. At the height of the conflict, 1.7 million people lived in these camps across the region. The conditions were squalid and there was no way for the people to make a living. As a result, a generation of Acholi people was born and raised in these camps.

Here's how bad it was. The UN had built toilets for the women, and were annoyed because the toilets had never been used. I said, "Do you know why they don't use them?"

"No."

"Because if women go to the toilets built in such an enclosed space at night, they get raped. They'd rather pee in a bucket than get raped by the ones who are supposed to protect them."

I got together with some friends and suggested we create a medical care organization that had nothing to do with government or religion. We'd gather a small, elite group of men and women—basically special forces people, ultra athletes and survival experts, people who wouldn't be scared to go anywhere in the world—and we'd just go out and provide good care and education with no strings attached. Two years ago we started applying for our licenses, and now Team 5 Foundation has a huge board of directors and has been recognized by Congress, the Senate, and the Green Beret Foundation, and has received two awards from the secretary of defense. T5 also holds the gold standard from Guidestar, the BBB of nonprofits.

In its first year, 2011, Team 5 did three missions in Belize and Guatemala. The second year we did Belize and Guatemala again, including the earthquake in San Marcos, Guatemala, by the request of the First Lady. This year we've done Guatemala, St. Vincent and the Grenadines, and just returned from Dominican Republic. We're limited only by funding, not the people we invite, because we have plenty of volunteers. It's the funding that's hardest, even though we use only about fifteen to twenty thousand dollars per mission— nothing when we bring over a million in donated medications and supplies plus teaching our curriculum to the local health providers.

We approach a mission in three parts. First we speak with the Ministry of Health at the location; then we figure out what their medical education level is; and then we teach a two-day advanced class. We bring all the supplies and build a core curriculum that's certified in the US. While the clinic people are attending class we take over the clinic so they can't claim they have nobody to help them. We usually end up teaching 25 to 40 people in advanced medicine while running their clinics for them.

For the next five days we run clinics in five different locations. We map out which locations have never been reached before, hire boat drivers and guides and porters and go out every day to a new location. It might take two hours to get there, whether by boat or on foot. We've gone through flash floods and earthquakes and everything you can think of to reach these locations. Our core group includes me; Dave, a special forces Green Beret medic; and Brigit, an ultra athlete and winner of the Jay Cutler Body Building Competition, who is also a pediatric intensive care nurse. All are volunteers.

When we get there we set up a makeshift clinic and see about 100 to 125 people per day. We could be doing anything from dental care, primary care, outpatient surgeries to ultrasounds, not to mention the kinds of injuries that might come in to any E.R. At the end of the day we break down and take everything to our base camp to resupply. The next day we go back out, and so on, back and forth until we're done with that area. The indigenous people will walk for days to get care when they hear we are going to be at a specific location. It's very humbling to be able to make someone feel better. On the last day all the supplies and medical equipment are donated to the practitioners we just helped teach so they have tools to use. We want them to be self-sufficient and sustainable.

We know the course works because we've gotten requests for more courses on subjects like emergency childbirth, suturing and wilderness medicine. The infant mortality rate for the Mayans and Guatemalans was high just because the way they delivered babies; we basically taught them the Western style of delivery and brought them one-time use sterile packs. Before we came to the region there were two childbirth deaths per day. We've been told this rate has reduced dramatically because of the kits we brought and the alternative delivery technique we taught the clinic personnel. The birthing kits are sterile, which reduces the chance of the mother and the baby getting an infection—the usual cause of death.

It's all about giving people a hand, giving back to the world. I was shown how important this is when I was in Israel. David Revivo, a Colonel in the Israeli Police, was the kind of guy who really believes in giving back. During the two years I was in Israel he taught me to care for the soldiers, and while I was a soldier he took care of me when I had no money. Being divorced with two small children, I sold my truck and everything I owned so I could maintain my financial obligations to the children. Metro wasn't paying me to be there, and the salary I was being paid by Israel was just enough for snacks and cigarettes. So David brought me in with this family, as his little brother. Later, when I became a regular soldier and was receiving a higher salary, I passed his tradition on by taking other soldiers under my wing. David guided me through this whole experience of giving back and using the skills you've learned in the military and police force in a positive way.

I also started giving back to Israel after I left my pararescue Unit. I have been approved to be a volunteer member of Mogan David Adom, Israel's equivalent to the Red Cross and I have been volunteering in the mobile intensive care unit. Because of my license I can go on the ambulance, which allows a doctor to stay in the emergency room, rather than being on the unit, which helps the emergency rooms. I've been volunteering for the Israeli Red Cross (MDA) for about eight years now, and that's the experience that led to the creation of Team 5. To this day, my relationship with David is that of brothers and we speak often. We belong to the same organization—an organization that helps people. I hope it continues to be contagious, and more and more people participate in doing something bigger than themselves. Not only is it the right thing to do, but it feels good to take the hurt away, even if I can reach only a handful of people.

The Team 5 motto: "In order to be involved, you must first show up," expresses the importance of doing more than talking about doing something great: you need to put both feet in.

"You never know when you're going to be in a crisis."

COLONEL HARVEY "BARNEY" BARNUM

Who is Barney Barnum? In late 1965, first lieutenant Harvey C. "Barney" Barnum Jr. arrived in Vietnam with the Ninth Marines. On the morning of December 18, his company of about 110 men was ambushed by a vastly larger force of North Vietnamese regulars and cut off from the rest of their battalion.

Barnum found the company commander mortally wounded and the radio operator killed—targeted by the enemy to destroy the marines' command and control. Disregarding his personal safety, Barnum gave aid to the dying commander, then removed the radio from the dead operator and strapped it to himself. Estimating that the enemy had the rifle company outnumbered by ten to one, he assumed command and moved at once into heavy fire, rallying, encouraging and reorganizing the decimated units. He called in an artillery attack, then directed First Platoon in a successful counterattack on the key enemy positions that were pinning his men down with machine gun fire.

After nearly eight hours of continuous fighting, the battalion commander radioed Barnum that they could not mount a rescue for his cut-off marines. Barnum ordered the company engineers to blow a space in trees so two helicopters could land and evacuate the dead and wounded. Then he had the rest of his men move out in fire team rushes against the enemy. Perhaps because the maneuver was so unexpected, the marines broke through the North Vietnamese lines and crossed 500 yards of fire-swept ground to rejoin forward elements of their battalion before darkness.

Two days later Barnum was told that he had been recommended for the Medal of Honor, which he later received.

For more information please visit **www.homeofheroes.com/ barney**.

•••

I was born on July 21, 1940, in Cheshire, Connecticut, a farming town located halfway between New York and Boston. It was a small town with a sheep and cattle farm up the street, a lot of chicken farms, produce and vegetables.

I grew up in that atmosphere and went to the same grammar school my mother attended. My mom was an orphan who'd been adopted by a professor at the Chesire Academy and lived in Cheshire most of her life. My father was born in Danbury, Connecticut—which is ironic because that's where P.T. Barnum grew up.

My parents were just great. We didn't have a lot, but we didn't want for anything. My dad worked three or four jobs, and Mom was a homemaker. Mom was a strong Irish Catholic lady, and I became an altar boy even though my dad was non-Catholic and not religious. I remember him driving me at 6:30 in the morning to Mass, waiting in the car, then taking Mom, my brother and me to church services, and picking us up afterward.

But my dad had been very active in scouting when he was a youngster, and I followed in those footsteps. Scouting agreed with me; I liked the discipline, the organization and teamwork, and being outdoors. I was a junior leader and became assistant bcout master. I went to California in 1953 to a Boy Scout Jamboree, then went to a convention in Indiana. In 1957 the town raised the money to send me to the Baden-Powell Jamboree in England.

At the time I was 17 and working as Chief of Order of the Arrow, which is an honors society in scouting. Years later I induced my father into going into the order as well. We did a lot of work at Scout Camp and were up there on weekends. When I played sports my father went to every one of my games. He was very involved in Little League and was an umpire for years, even after I left for college. I don't know how he did it all, but he did.

He was even a volunteer fireman. My dad never said curse words nor had tolerance for people who swore in front of his wife—and you can imagine how rough the language could be around the firehouse. Many times I saw my father call guys aside—including the chief—and remind them that there were ladies on deck . . . and more importantly, his wife was on deck. Everyone respected my father. He handled all the books at the firehouse, and ran their fund drives. As a result I was around the fire department a lot, which led to me becoming a volunteer firemen when I was 18.

One day when I was home from college, we got a call about a barn fire. Dad and I were the first ones there, but the cops brought us back to get an old ambulance to bring the water pump down. We were driving it through the center of town and saw traffic ahead.

My father said, "Where's the goddamned siren on this thing?"

I was shocked. "Dad, I never heard you swear before!"

"That's right. So where's the goddamned siren?"

Mom was a great homemaker and discipline was big in our home, but we lived by the Golden Rule. Between home, church and scouting I gained an understanding of how important it is to think of your fellow man—service before self, not all I, I, I, me, me, me. My upbringing was all about "love your fellow man" and "do the right thing at the right time for the right reasons." The town, the quality of its people, church, Boy Scouts, my mom and dad—all that became the foundation on which I built my life.

I tell kids today that every action has a reaction. Before you make a decision, consider what your mom and dad would think about it, or your grandma and grandpa. I didn't want to do anything that would disappoint or hurt my parents. Whenever I got in a little mischief and saw their reaction, how disappointed they were and now upset I'd gotten them, I felt terrible. I didn't want to do that.

My father used to tell me that when you make up your mind about doing something, give it 100% or don't do it. Be disciplined and motivated, take on a task and do it and get it done. My reward has been to see that work. You never know when you're going to be in a crisis.

Once when I was on a Boy Scout canoe trip on a river, I saw a guy in a cove waving his arms. There were six or seven boats in our group, and I told them I was going over to check on the man. It turned out his lady had passed out. She was diabetic, short of sugar, and turning blue.

I got out of my canoe, climbed into his boat, started the motor and asked the man if he had sugar. He said no. I knew sugar was what she needed , so I asked the man where his lunch was. He pointed to a picnic area. We motored over there and I shouted, "Who has sugar? I've got a diabetic here and she needs sugar!"

People gave me jars of sugar. I got in the water, held the woman's mouth open and forced her to swallow sugar. At that time state troopers showed up and carried her out of the boat, but she was still not with us. They put her in back of a car. I got in, and the woman's boyfriend climbed in front with the trooper, and we were off to a doctor's office.

The woman was successfully revived. For me it was a case of do the right thing at the right time for the right reasons.

When I was a senior in high school we had a career day. All the services had representatives there in an auditorium full of junior and senior boys. The boys made rude jokes and catcalls when the air force guy got up to speak, and the same with the navy and the army. Then the marine corps speaker got up. He said, "There's no one in this room I want in my marine corps. You're undisciplined." He chewed out the faculty in the back of the room for letting the kids get out of hand, packed up his gear and walked offstage.

He was folding up his brochures when thirteen guys came to his table and signed up for the marine corps. I was one of them. I joined to become an officer, get my feet on the ground, grow up a little, see the world, and then get on with life.

That was in 1958. I'd spend the next thirty years as a marine—part of it, of course, in Vietnam.

Someone asked me how I felt when I received the Medal of Honor around my neck. At the time I was looking right at my mom and dad. I saw the tears and pride in their eyes, and I said, "I finally paid you back."

"Just ringing the bell and being the lone voice of reason in the wilderness helps."

NIGER INNIS

Who is Niger Innis? Niger Innis is the national spokesman for the Congress of Racial Equality (CORE) and the former chief strategist for TheTeaParty.net. Mr. Innis is also involved with Affordable Power Alliance (APA), a coalition of Latino and African American ministerial organizations; Senior Citizen Advocates, which fights against public policies that raise energy (and associated) costs; Advisory Committee Project 21 for the National Center for Public Policy Research; is a consultant to EEN247.com, Empowerment and Excellence cable channel; and serves on the NRA Membership Committee. In December of 2012, Niger co-founded the New America organization with Julie Hereford, Victor Chaltiel, Carlo Maffat and Leo Bletnitsky.

During the 1993 New York City Democratic Party primary, Niger served as campaign manager for the Roy Innis mayoral campaign and helped to garner more than 25% of the vote. In 1997 he served as a delegate to the 19th American-German Young Leaders Conference and was later selected by senior US leaders to serve on the American Delegation to the American Swiss Foundation Young Leaders Conference in Switzerland.

Niger's civil rights and political activities led to television and radio appearances around the world. He was hired as a political and social commentator for MSNBC and for National Public Radio. He has also been a guest on CNN, BBC, CBC, Al-Jeezera, Fox News Channel, ABC News, CBS News, etc. Niger is currently a commentator for NBC News in his adopted home state of Nevada.

For more information please visit **www.core-online.org**.

•••

I was born in the Bronx on March 5th, 1968, but my dad, mom and I moved to Harlem when I was two. I grew up in the area called Strivers Row, which was once the elite of elites of uptown communities. Even in my childhood it was an upper- to middle-class community; our neighbors were doctors, historians, librarians—professional people at the tops of their fields.

Therefore I grew up around a group of extraordinary black Americans who achieved a great deal in their lives. I was also blessed to attend the Cathedral of St. John the Divine, one of the elite Episcopalian schools in the country, where I gained my affections for God and Christianity. My mom was an atheist and my dad an agnostic, but this was the early seventies, so of course I followed the cultural trend and rebelled against my parents by believing in God and Christ.

At that time maybe five percent of the people attending St. John the Divine were black—no doubt a huge increase from the year before. There were also a few Asian-American and Latino kids—but it was a predominantly white institution. Still, classmates came to my house and I went to their houses; there were birthday parties and sleepovers, all kinds of stuff. My classmates even elected me governor of one of the American colonies during a mock history lesson of early American Colonial history.

At the same time, this was Harlem in the 1970s—which was not the same as in 2013. There were crack dens two blocks from my neighborhood. There were gunshots at night and even during the day, and they happened often enough that we had a procedure: "If you hear a pop, you drop." It was scary as hell, but still, I'm thankful I had that experience. Because of it I'm not a spoiled brat, an upper-class kid. I had balance in my life, and that balance has given me a great deal of enrichment over the years.

I was also enriched by my friendships. Back then some of my dearest friends were from the 'hood, but others were schoolmates who lived in wonderful places. This taught me that in contemporary America there is no such thing as a caste system. Doesn't exist. I've met too many good white, bad black, great Latino, awful Asian, terrible rich and wonderful poor people to put a stereotype on anybody. *Diversity* was my experience growing up.

Of course, my father was and is a Black Nationalist. I hear you thinking: Wait a minute, isn't your father the same Roy Innis who dumped Al Sharpton on his butt? The same Roy Innis who's one of the most prominent black conservatives in the country? But isn't "Black Nationalism" what the Nation of Islam preaches, or the Black Panthers? Aren't Black Nationalists just crazy cooks who want to burn everything down?

No. That might be to some extent an accurate projection of what the media and academicians *say* Black Nationalism is, but *real* Black Nationalism goes as far back as Marcus Garvey.

Garvey was a Jamaican-American man who came to this country in the early twentieth century and combined the self-help philosophy of Booker T. Washington with industrialized behavior and a fierce desire to end colonialism around the world. At that time Africa was cut up like a pizza pie amongst European powers. You had French West Africa; British West Africa; and North Africa, which was almost entirely a French colony. Egypt was controlled by the British in a semi-colonial relationship.

America was also a different place then. We were a different kind of country, and black people were different. At the time, to call someone black was insulting. And I'm not talking about a white person calling a black person black; it was considered an insult for a *black* person to call anyone else black.

Keep in mind that at the time we were only a few decades out of slavery, a time when of course blacks were at the bottom of the economic barrel. Slightly above them were mixed-race blacks, but even then not every child who came from a union between a white man and a black woman was abandoned. Although at the time having an open relationship with your half-black child was cutting against the social custom, former Senator Strom Thurmond (now deceased) himself financially supported his mulatto daughter. Later, when she was asked if she hated her father for what he did, she said, "No, I love this man to death. I've always known who he was and he's always been a part of my life."

In those circumstances you had an almost *de facto* racial caste—a separate caste of mixed children. But again, many of those children had the opportunity to go to good schools; in fact, some of the original black colleges were established especially for these kids.

Given this caste system with whites at the top, mulatto or mixed-race blacks in the middle, and blacks themselves at the bottom, you can understand how blacks came to feel about themselves. And of course it all started with slavery and segregation, with white racism—but inevitably we black people adopted those values and perceptions and promoted them *ourselves.*

Garvey wanted to cut against that. He wanted a free and independent Africa that would give blacks around the world something positive to look at and stop thinking that their whole existence is based upon being a former slave or descended from slaves. That was Garvey's vision, and my father agreed with it, so he took on the mantle and called himself a "Garviette."

Of course, nationalism of any sort can cross the border to become anti-somebody else. It can become extremism, like with the Kaiser who helped make Germany a world power at the turn of the twentieth century. That was German nationalism, and of course it had its most extreme manifestation in Adolf Hitler and Nazism. But while Nationalism and Nazism might have been cousins, they weren't the same things. I would compare my father's Black Nationalism to the Kaiser mentality. It wasn't anti-white or anti-Latino, it was just pro-black.

The Nation of Islam, on the other hand, isn't just pro-black; it's pro-Islam, with Muslim Arabic people as their top of the line. If you saw a picture of Elijah Mohammed, who created the Nation of Islam, you'd think he was a white man.

On top of that they have this mythology that the evil white man created racism. I met somebody—a white guy, actually—

who grew up with the Black Panthers, and I asked him how he would define Black Nationalism. When he brought up the Nation of Islam, I said, "How about the Black Panthers?"

He said, "No way. The Black Panthers? They're just a bunch of thugs who picked up a communist philosophy. They wore black clothes and they certainly were anti-white in some circumstances, and they were appreciated in the community—but they were not Black Nationalists." If you want to look at *real* Black Nationalism, he told me, look at Marcus Garvey.

Similarly, on another occasion an Irish Catholic priest—an older fellow who worked in Harlem—came up to me and said, "I grew up around that Garvey. I was a little boy, and you know something? He was never hostile to whites."

But the pendulum can swing too far in the other direction, too. That happened even with my father's brand of Black Nationalism: certain manifestations of it, corruptions of it, were a little chauvinistic—not racist but *chauvinistic*, simply putting people in boxes.

But my personal experiences growing up cut against that. For example, one day while I was going to Cathedral I saw a black kid, one of my fellow students, fighting with a white kid. They were getting hot, and my Black Nationalist instincts compelled me to get behind my brother. So I joined the fight.

Two white kids jumped me, and one started choking me out. Later I found out that while that was going on, a white kid I knew, Chris Powell, jumped out to get the other white boys off me— while my black brother ran away from the scene. He didn't help me; Chris Powell helped me.

What I learned was that with Chris, it wasn't about being black or white, it was about backing up Niger, my buddy. To make matters worse, I found out the black kid started the fight in the first place. I'd chosen sides based on skin color, and that wasn't fair.

Chris gave me a great education that day, but that was only the start. Meeting people throughout my life has shown me the importance of not stereotyping, not making assumptions based upon the package.

By the time I left Cathedral, CORE had created a community school. CORE stands for Congress of Racial Equality. It's one of the "Big Four" civil rights organizations, along with the NAACP, the Urban League, and SCLS. If you ever saw the movie *Mississippi Burning*, which was based on a true story from the civil rights era, you'll remember three college boys—two whites and one black—being murdered by the Klan for registering a black person to vote. These boys were engaged in a CORE project; they lost their lives as CORE workers. So we're one of the classic civil rights organizations, one of the oldest in the country.

I joined the CORE school, even though at that time it was just a single classroom. That was quite an experience: all black kids, all working class. A year after that I went to Wagner Jr. High, which was a different kind of diversity experience: a community school attended by whites, Latinos (largely Dominicans). That should tell you a lot about the diversity of bigotry. Dominicans come in different colors: some are virtually white and some are as black as me, but they have this vision of themselves as being neither black nor white: they are *Dominican.*

Yet the phenomenon of a color caste existed in the Dominican Republic, too. The Dominicans at school had a word for me: "*mocheco.*" These were some of my best buds, but that word means "nigger." That was my first semi-adult case of discrimination. I loved those guys and they loved me, too; we were very tight friends, so when one of them called me *mocheco,* I said, "Robert, you're darker than me, your hair is kinkier than mine, and you're calling *me mocheco?*"

He goes, "Aw, the Dominican is very hot; I just got a tan."

And that's how this son of a Black Nationalist discovered that the Dominicans didn't care if you were brown or black: we were brothers, we were *compadres,* in spite of their racism.

Obviously CORE is a black organization, and we help the black community, but more importantly we're an *American* organization and an *American* community. When the turbulent '60s came to an end, visionaries like my father could see that the country was changing; the old struggles like slavery weren't solved, but they were on their way toward being solved. My dad used to tell me that it shook him when he saw President Lyndon Baines Johnson with his Southern drawl say a phrase from the civil rights marchers: "We Shall Overcome." It moved him enough to decide we were turning a page on this whole black/white paradigm, this whole *de facto* law of segregation in the South.

Although there were certainly still problems in the community that had their roots in racism, they weren't being *perpetuated* because of racism. Therefore simply ending racism wouldn't fix those problems. It wouldn't stop black-on-black crime. It wouldn't put a dent in drug addiction, or welfare dependency, or the negative self-image that still exists with many blacks.

So my father decided to change the trajectory of CORE, to focus on fighting and beating those problems. At the time, the late '60s and early '70s, we were lonely voices insisting that crime, not racism but *crime,* was the biggest problem in the black community. My father insisted on not apologizing for crime or claiming that committing crimes should be excused because of racism. "Forget racism," he said. "Crime is the real problem."

In my opinion my father laid the platform for Rudy Guliani that created a revolution in New York City and had a domino effect throughout our country in terms of fighting crime. That revolution affected not only New York City and urban America, but *all* of America. And in the process it helped save the lives of thousands or even tens of thousands of people who are trapped in these communities.

I give my father and CORE credit for being pioneers in taking on that battle, although even today crime and explaining crime remain amongst the biggest problems we face. We have a victimization syndrome in the black community according to which racism explains everything: the dropout rate and the low graduation rate, the gap in academic achievement, black-on-black crime. *I'm a victim, I'm a victim.*

The problem is that even though that attitude might give you comfort in the short run, in the long run it cripples you. It prevents you from coldly analyzing what the problems are and how to solve them instead of focusing on this big fog of racism that simply creates paralysis.

CORE cut back against that—which obviously put us at odds with a lot of civil rights establishment. Under my father's leadership, CORE became quite a different organization than, say, the national NAACP did. Back in the early '70s the NAACP would probably have embraced the anti-victim syndrome my father championed, but instead, tragically, it came to embrace the victim syndrome instead. That's how guys like Al Sharpton, who the NAACP would have probably laughed at back at the beginning of his career, has become a mainstream leader of the civil rights establishment.

And that's a tragedy. Not because of Al, personally, but because his philosophy on racism creates paralysis for not only our country as a whole, but for the very community we're trying to help. What we should be saying to young folks is, "Hey, look—yes, your grandparents and your great-grandparents were victims of racism, profound racism; but their sacrifices forced this country to change. You now have opportunities they never did—what are our responsibilities to maximize those opportunities?

That's the message we should be getting out to our children, but it's not the message the Shockleys and the Jesse Jacksons and the Congressional Black Caucuses are putting out. Even the President of the United States, the most visible beneficiary of the changes we're speaking of, even he—and I say this with deep, deep sadness—doesn't deliver that message. He would be the perfect role model if he'd just say, "No more excuses. Here are the things that need to be done in the new America. We now have a country that isn't just blacks and whites but also Latinos and Asian-Americans and blacks from other countries competing with you, and if you don't have certain skills and certain values you're going to lose this race. So what can we do to help empower you to be competitive in that race?"

That was my father's mission and remains the mission of CORE today. I see us as pioneers.

My father is one of my heroes. I got many of my political beliefs, especially on race relations and openness to the Republican Party, from my dad. In 1972 he was called the "lone black Dick Nixon supporter," and I've also always been open to Republican politics and philosophies. If my mom taught me how to feel like an American, my father taught me how to *think* like an American. He was an immigrant. A lot of immigrants come to this country without believing that whites are racists who owe them something. They come with optimism and drive. *The streets aren't quite paved with gold*, these people think, *but they're damned close compared to where I came from, and now I have an opportunity to take advantage of it.* That's the way most Americans think.

But not everyone. I grew up in Harlem in the 1980s, so I watched the birth of rap music. Back then rap was harmless in comparison to a lot of the garbage today, but still, the music celebrated certain social pathologies. Rap music should be poetry, should be something to uplift and expose, to tell the truth and help solve problems. Instead it celebrated the gangster life, promoting what I call a "criminal chic," where being a gangster or criminal is cool and the drug dealer is a role model.

What about the kid flipping hamburgers at McDonald's? If he passes on using drugs he's considered a nerd, a loser. So to be a black role model you have to be a drug dealer, a thug or a pimp.

I saw the future back then, and I was right. I called it part of the "entertainment/ industrial complex," and I still see it as a clear and present danger to blacks and other minorities, and American progress in general. Rap is now a multibillion dollar industry that's made millionaires out of whites and blacks and others. On the other hand, it's like how drug use starts in one community and eventually spills over into other communities— that's what's happening in the white community right now. If you go to an all-white suburb you'll see kids wearing saggy pants and caps turned backward.

We've got an integrated, interdependant society where both positive and negative cultural influences get elaborated. What values does rap music promote? Think about it. Here's a kid in the inner city. His mom is single and dad is not in the home. His mom works two or three jobs to keep food on the table, so she's never home either. So there's the kid, watching TV by himself and feeding into his brain some the worst messages, the worst morals, the worst values and the worst role models you could possibly imagine. The entertainment industry becomes a surrogate parent to that child—a kid who doesn't have the positive tools I was talking about. In fact he has *negative* tools; he has tools to take him down the pathway to prison or a graveyard.

CORE fights this trend, first of all, by simply raising the issue. My first debate on Black Entertainment Television twenty years ago was with Sister Souljah and dealt with these types of questions. So just ringing the bell and being the lone voice of reason in the wilderness helps. And to my pleasant surprise, over the decades there's been some penetration: now even Al Sharpton gives lip service, at least, to stuff like this.

Not long ago I was on Sean Hannity's show with Jesse Jackson's daughter, and I was critiquing the president for not only failing to take on the industrial/entertainment complex, but for empowering it. His BFF is Jay-Z! Look, I'm all for success stories, and God bless Jay-Z for the economic prosperity that's come his way—but the difference between him and Malcolm X is this: while both were drug dealers, Malcolm X totally repudiated that part of himself. He said that as a drug dealer he had been a plague on the black community. Sure, he blamed white folks for making him that way, but he also admitted that that was in the past; he turned the page on it.

On the other hand, Jay-Z is an unrepentant drug dealer who still raps about dealing. When he was dealing he liked to call himself a "pharmacist delivering a service to a community in pain."

President Obama was brought to power largely because folks were saying, "Finally we've got a black leader who can be a role model, who's good for the country, and we can turn the page on racism and these negative role models . . . " So when the president says his BFF is Jay-Z, that cuts against the message. If I'm a little kid in Harlem I'd say, *Man, even the Ivy League-educated President of the United States is communicating with Jay-Z! I want to be like Jay-Z!*

Fortunately that was never the situation for me. My mother was a very proud black American woman who, to my father's regret, instilled American patriotism into me (he always wanted me to consider myself a West-Indian). But her influence gave me a pride in and ownership of this country that no white person or other black person can take away. Mom was my first hero, even though we argued from the time since I was little boy. She was a liberal, but also a very proud black American—and I deliberately use the term "black American" instead of "African American." Although I'm comfortable with either term, for me "black American" is better. More specific. Barack Obama is truly an "African American" because his father was African and his mother was a white American, born and raised in this country.

But most black Americans' ancestry traces back to slavery, to Alabama, Kentucky, Texas, Georgia—and that's a different experience. 2019 will mark the 400th year that blacks have been in this/these country/colonies; the first slave got off the ship in 1619. Our blood—literally, our blood, sweat and tears—is embedded in this country and in American culture. Cherishing that reality came from my mother to me; she taught me a large part of who I am.

Another hero for me is Justice John Marshall Harlan, a white man and the lone dissenter in the infamous *Plessy vs. Ferguson* decision of 1896—the "separate but equal" decision that for a half-century would be used to justify segregation throughout the South until it was overturned by the *Brown vs. Board of Education* decision. Harlan's dissent was fascinating, firstly because of who he was—a white Southerner and former slave owner from Kentucky. In his dissent he said that whites were at the top of the social ladder because of their achievements and values and would stay there—if not forever, then for a very long time. But he added that the Constitution does not recognize racial or social castes. According to the Constitution, the most powerful among us are the same as the lowest. We are a nation of law and rules, not a nation of castes. So, Harlan said, I'm not against segregation because I love black people or because I'm superior to black people or because I want to be nice to black people. I'm against segregation because it's unconstitutional!

For someone back then to have that type of vision was amazing. Harlan was not an abolitionist. The abolitionists of his time were the radicals. They wanted to help black folk and they intermarried with black folk, so God bless them, they had a mission and they had a strong belief in God. But Harlan was not one of them. His agenda was to be true the Constitution and to what made America what it is. To me that is just a splendid example; I took it to heart and it's been a part of my philosophy ever since.

But my biggest ideological hero and role model is Booker T. Washington, an ex-slave who picked himself up by his own bootstraps. He had confidence in his race and confidence in his country, and believed that blacks would be like any other ethnic group if we'd pull up our sleeves and put a little sweat equity into it. His great Atlanta speech of 1896 will go down as one of the greatest speeches in history. And his roadmap for the success of the black community was emulated by both the Irish and the Italian immigrants who came into the country and were also discriminated against. There was a caste system then, and they were at the bottom of it.

But they took the high road of industrial education and perfecting trades, and of turning those trades into businesses, then turning those businesses into capital and development, and finally leveraging their economic capital into political power. Which was exactly the roadmap Booker T. Washington laid out for black America in 1896.

Unfortunately, at that same time progressivism was coming to fruition in our country, and cutting radically against those ideas. Still, Booker T. Washington was, is, and will always be, a huge hero of mine. I believe he walked the right path for anyone—not just blacks—who want to be successful in the USA.

"I put the needs of my crew first."

MIKE ABRASHOFF

Who is Mike Abrashoff? At the age of 36, Mike Abrashoff was selected by the US Navy to become commander of *USS Benfold*—which made him the most junior commanding officer in the Pacific Fleet at the time. The immediate challenges that faced him were staggering: exceptionally low morale with unacceptably high turnover. Few thought that this ship could improve.

Mike's solution was to establish a system of management techniques that he calls the Leadership Roadmap, a process of replacing command and control with commitment and cohesion by engaging the hearts, minds, and loyalties of workers. "It's your ship," he was known to say.

These principles achieved breakthrough results. Personnel turnover decreased to an unprecedented one percent; the rate of military promotions tripled; and the crew slashed operating expenses by 25 percent. Eventually regarded as the finest ship in the Pacific Fleet, Benfold won the prestigious Spokane Trophy for having the highest degree of combat readiness.

Mike recounted the leadership lessons from his turnaround of *USS Benfold* in the *New York Times* best-selling book *It's Your Ship*. For more information please visit **www.glsworld.com**.

•••

I grew up in a small town in Pennsylvania as the sixth of seven kids in a middle- to lower middle-class family. I went off to the Naval Academy, graduated, and was assigned to surface ships in the US Navy.

When I came up through the ranks there was a saying: "We eat our young." It was a tough environment where people don't spend much time building you up, but do a great job of tearing you down.

Still, I climbed up through the ranks, and in the summer of 1994 I was selected to be the junior military assistant to the secretary of defense, Dr. William Perry. He turned out to be a person who changed the course of my life. It wasn't so much that he was charismatic or even outgoing. Instead he was a genuine and authentic leader, a person who treated you with respect and dignity. A person who listened to you.

When I got there I was a minor figure in the office under a two-star army general, a senior military assistant—the same job Colin Powell had when he was a two-star. Four of the civilians working in the office were the equivalent of four-star admirals, very smart and capable people . . . and then here I came. I felt insecure at first, thinking I didn't deserve to be with such an elite group of people. So I just kept my head down and did my job every day. I wasn't in a leadership position; I was an individual contributor.

But at first I wasn't all that effective with my job, which made me angry at myself. Why couldn't I figure out how to become better at what I was doing? Finally I decided to simply observe everything the two-star general did. Every decision he made, every piece of paper that he thought was important enough to send over to the secretary of defense, I made sure to know why. Over time I trained myself to think like the two-star. Before he made a decision I'd try to put myself in his shoes and anticipate what his decision would be. If he concluded the same thing I had, I figured I was on the right track. But if he made a different decision, it meant something was wrong with my thought process or my training; there was something I needed to fix. By my definition, the general and the secretary of defense are always right!

I adapted my thinking style for them. I watched the general like a hawk: every decision he made, I tried to anticipate his needs. He was working 14-15 hours a day, so I wanted to lift burdens off his shoulders. Over time he learned to trust me, and started to give me some of his responsibilities so he'd have time to be of better service to the secretary of defense.

Up until then I was still an individual contributor, doing my job but leading no one, supervising no one. But then the general gave me responsibility to oversee the trip planning team, which comprised 25 people. Then I took charge of the security detail, which was another 25 people, followed by the communications team, which was 40-50 people. He gave me a job that my predecessors, many of whom went on to make admiral or general, never did. Suddenly I was in a leadership position.

After about 14 months of this I was feeling good about myself. I was working hard and felt like I was making a difference. But then the general's son got sick and almost died, so the general didn't work for a month and a half. During those 45 days I had to do both his job and my own—and it went without a hitch because I'd prepared myself to step into his shoes if necessary.

When the general's son recovered and the general came back to work, he went in to see the secretary of defense. They didn't realize I was standing at the door listening to their conversation as the general asked Dr. Perry how I'd done in his absence. Dr. Perry looked up from his desk and said, "He did great. I consider you and him interchangeable."

The general's shoulders slumped because he was being compared to a low-life navy commander. But my chest puffed out. I'd grown up in the navy where we spent most of the time tearing people down, and now Dr. Perry had given me validation that said, *Hey, you're a good person and you can do the work, you can play in the big leagues.*

It changed the way I looked at my career. I never had to get promoted again, because I knew I could do the job of a one- or two-star general. That confidence alleviated the need for me to have to constantly put my own career and my own needs first. I knew I could do the job, so I decided to just focus on results and people; I put the needs of my crew first. They came to trust me, and we became a tight-knit, cohesive unit of 310 people—all because I no longer needed to worry about my career.

It was Dr. William Perry who gave me that validation, who gave me the confidence to do the great things we did years later when I was assigned to the *USS Benford.*

This was a man who had a Ph.D. in mathematics and was an engineering professor at Stanford. He'd started a company that employed 1,500 to 2,000 people and would eventually be bought by PRW—yet he dedicated his life to national security and the defense of his country. He's the father of stealth technology, one of the researchers who did the mathematical equations showing how to evade enemy radar. Tomahawk cruise missiles were created on his watch, starting in the late 1970s. He had the foresight to nurture all these revolutionary systems, get funding for them and bring them online.

I once asked him what his biggest mistake was, and he told me about something that happened during the Carter administration when he was under secretary of defense for research and engineering. At that time the country was having budget trouble, and one of the programs they tried to zero out was the Geostationary Positioning System, or GPS. Most people don't realize that GPS began as a system of military satellites that covers the entire globe. Dr. Perry went to the Senate Armed Services Committee and begged them not to cut the funding for the project, even though he had no idea just how important GPS would become.

The committee listened. So what was the failure? For Dr. Perry, it was not anticipating what GPS would eventually be able to do and figuring out a way to charge users for access to the system. If he'd done that, he would have been able to fund the entire DOD budget with nothing but GPS user fees!

Despite all his accomplishments, you could be a janitor in the halls of the Pentagon, you could be a private, and he would treat you the same way he treated the chairman of Department of Defense staff. He touched thousands of lives because he knew that the simple act of validation gives people the confidence to go out and do great things.

He didn't inspire me to write a book, but he inspired me to do the things I wrote about in my book. And when he wrote a book of his own I was honored that he mentioned me in it as being a valuable assistant to him as well.

"I try to empower the talents of others to shine, and, by shining,
to enlighten the dark corners of the mind and the world."

JONATHAN WYGANT

Who is Jonathan Wygant? Jonathan Wygant is CEO and founder of BigSpeak, Inc., the largest business-oriented agency/consultancy in North America focused on serving the Fortune 1000 and multinational companies worldwide. BigSpeak addresses the needs of corporations, associations, nonprofits and government agencies by providing inspirational speakers, thought leaders and subject matter experts.

Jonathan draws on his more than 30 years of hands-on business experience and extensive research into the best practices of visionary leaders and successful companies. His expertise is in understanding his client's needs and matching them with speakers and trainers who will best deliver inspirational messages and support lasting positive organizational change.

Before founding BigSpeak, Jonathan was the CEO and co-founder of Iris Arc Crystal, an Inc. 500 international giftware manufacturing company headquartered in Santa Barbara, CA.

He is a member of the World Presidents' Organization (WPO) and a board member of SuperSprings International as well as the

International Association of Speakers Bureaus, and worked as a board member with the organization Heal the Ocean. Jonathan received a bachelor of arts in English with an economics minor at Hamilton College and a master of arts in applied psychology, University of Santa Monica.

For more information please visit **www.bigspeak.com**.

•••

A third-generation Californian, I grew up cherishing the raw, dry, red-earthed beauty of Southern California. My father, Benyaurd, worked in the defense industry, moving from place to place with the ease of an expert, in demand with companies like General Dynamics and McDonald Douglas. With every move to a new school, I adapted to new neighborhoods, new classmates, new teachers. I also became as familiar with the low desert landscape as other boys were with their own backyards.

Yet in search of a college degree I chose Hamilton College in upstate New York, a lovely old-world campus with roots dating back to 1793. Then, with an BA in English under my belt, I spent a year and a half in Europe, working at three jobs that taught me more about people and life than any pastoral college class.

I really didn't know what I wanted to do after college. But I knew I'd had enough of book learning, so I travelled throughout Europe, meeting all sorts of people from different backgrounds and economic strata. This experience helped me figure out who I was as distinct from my family background, values or prejudices.

And I worked and played hard. I managed a hamburger stand in Spain, was the night porter and assistant bartender in a Swiss hotel, and worked as a dishwasher at the officers' club at the Ramstein Air Force Base in Germany. I was always learning, observing and experiencing new things. I wanted to craft my soul, like an Argonaut.

This desire to become my fullest self continued after I returned from my travels, so I kept up my experimental employment until I encountered my first real job opportunity: to serve as a social worker at Sonoma State Hospital in Northern California. It was extremely challenging work. Twelve months later I took to the road again, only to come back to Southern California as if drawn by a magnet. That was when I co-founded my first company, Iris Arc Crystal, in 1976.

I was fortunate. We launched at the crest of the crystal phenomenon. Up until that time, beautiful, faceted crystals were found only on the chandeliers of the wealthy, not hanging in windows casting rainbows around the rooms of humble homes. It was almost as if I had found the end of my personal rainbow. The business thrived, with sales doubling every year for five years. Everything we touched turned golden. At its peak, Iris Arc Crystal had 5,000 accounts and was listed as an Inc. 500 company. With products sold in many department stores and virtually every Hallmark outlet, Iris Arc provided crystal prisms, jewelry, and figurines for almost every home in America, from coast to coast, for two decades.

Once, when sales were off during a recession, we created a wonderful service project called the Arc Angels. Instead of laying people off, we asked ourselves, "What good can we can do?" So we worked for four days each week, and then, on the fifth day, we paid our employees to do service projects throughout Santa Barbara. We reached out, calling Catholic Social Services, the Therapeutic Riding Academy as well as other groups, asking what needed to be done. Every Friday for several weeks, we completed service projects for those in need. Because of our community outreach, someone nominated our company for an important award.

With a sense of wonder, I found that Iris Arc Crystal had received a prestigious award to be given out by President Reagan. It was called the "We Can, We Care" award. I was astonished by this response to a few months of selfless service. Luminaries from successful firms packed the White House. We were probably the smallest company there. I sat next to Bill Marriott and actually met President Reagan and gave him a special crystal gift that ended up on Nancy Reagan's desk. Today, you could never bring gifts into the White House the way that I did back in the '80s. It was a great experience!

But after establishing Iris Arc as a success and building its international presence, I was ready for my next adventure. I sold Iris Crystal to one of our employees and took six months off to once again explore the world and myself. A year later I was at Esalen Institute, a wonderful personal growth center in the Big Sur area. While taking a workshop from Dr. Joan Borysenko, a renowned body-mind-spirit expert, I had a vision to develop a marketing organization focused on people's personal and professional development. I would offer speakers and thought leaders to conferences and corporations so these experts and teachers could educate and inspire while I handled the sales and marketing. The concept fell into my consciousness like a gift.

At breakfast the next morning, the vision coalesced. Joan wanted to be the first person I represented. She wanted to introduce me to other industry leaders, people she knew and trusted, people she had worked with for years. Within a month I received a letter from Joan with the contact information for experts from Deepak Chopra to John Gray, wonderful people with whom Joan had collaborated in the past who worked with integrity and heart.

This was the beginning of a new world for me. I gathered a core group of great individuals, of experts that specialized in helping people with personal growth, self-esteem and all kinds of personal and professional development. I marketed their services. Now, the company is known as BigSpeak, Inc. We schedule speaking and training for top experts focused on leadership, team building, change management, strategy, innovation and peak performance. On average, we have at least one speaker speaking somewhere on the planet every day of the year!

Today, BigSpeak has served the world for nearly 19 years. According to our records, the experts we represent have taught a variety of essential skills to over 2 million people in over 60% of the Fortune 1000, a broad spectrum of humanity. Many companies have been touched. Many individuals have had their lives changed for the better.

The legacy I've left is one that involves people, and that's something that can't be measured. It gives me a warm feeling to know that my focus is on giving and lifting, not just on selling. Sometimes you can't help but worry about the bills. But, most of the time we are focused and aware that we are in the business of wisdom provision. We are agents for speakers that are the resources of great practical knowledge, the kind that can't be found in traditional academic environments.

As I review my accomplishments so far, I can see that I have been a catalyst for change and growth. I work most of the time in the background. I try to empower the talents of others to shine, and, by shining, to enlighten the dark corners of the mind and the world. I enjoy contributing to the uplifting of humanity. Like the crystals I sold that scattered beautiful rainbows into darkened corners, BigSpeak enlightens people, as individuals and as groups, shining wisdom through eloquent, inspiring and practical words.

Regardless of my hopes, at first I didn't know how people were being affected by BigSpeak. I didn't get much feedback; still, the speakers hit the ball out of the park. We, as agents, were one step removed from the learning experience, but our speakers were on home plate. They heard people saying, "Wow! You really had an impact on our people's views and their ability to improve." This type of testimonial made all the difference when it came to leaving a legacy that really mattered!

The high caliber of speakers that we represent wasn't easy to find. I connected with them in many different ways: through hearing them in person, through meeting planners and enthused executives or through influential connections. Often, I read their stories or books. It gives me a warm feeling inside to know that my legacy includes raising the bar in the corporate world.

In many respects, corporations rule the world these days. If we can help these organizations be more aware of how they use natural resources to create meaningful products, of how to empower, educate and take care of their people, I think we'll leave a better world for future generations.

I also knew that if the corporate powers-that-be felt they had to worry about quarterly profits, our experts could address that issue by inspiring and empowering employees at all levels to further innovate and lead, a grassroots way to contribute to a vital economic challenge.

Throughout these adult successes, I have maintained a connection with my early dreams, hopes, and mentors. My first mentor was Alan Hunter, a Presbyterian minister in Los Angeles. He presided at the marriage ceremony of my parents, and married my sister and her spouse, long after baptizing me into the faith. His was a gentle yet strengthening presence. He radiated wisdom, and told me on several occasions that he lived his life with one foot in prayer and one foot in service. The prayer was to build positivity, to draw near to truth and stay connected to Spirit. The service was to say, "OK. Once I get that great idea or inspiration, I'll take the time to do something with it, to be of service and give unto others." These messages, received from humble Alan Hunter, left their mark.

I revere the memory of this quiet yet powerful man, and recall his influence with deep affection. I remember having time with him when my grandfather died, having time with him when I was baptized and confirmed, having time with him when I was in my early twenties. Once he retired to Pilgrim Place, we would visit. I remember that my friend, Larry Bartle, and I had a really good talk about mystical experiences, about being connected to wisdom at a level deeper than one's intellect. Alan Hunter had several significant impacts on my life over a two decade period. These were challenging times for me. But, they were also pivotal times, too, when my heart and mind were soft and open to new ways of embracing life.

I lost both of my grandfathers within a six month period. Alan had such a great quality. He was such a loving and caring person. He cared enough to pass something special on to me. His kindness gave me a place to be heard, a safe harbor during the storm. Yet, at some point, that same kindness gave me my marching orders, too.

The next mentor that impacted my life was John Roger, a spiritual teacher and founder of the Movement of Spiritual Inner Awareness (MSIA). He is a uniquely loving man who has amazing wisdom, beyond anything that I had ever experienced before. He reads the Akashic records of previous lives we have lived. He teaches the ability to meditate, to understand why certain things are happening in this life and to connect directly to one's soul. I rejoice in the radiance of John Roger's expanded being to this day.

One experience I had with John Roger was very helpful when I started my first business, Iris Arc. My partner and I had thought of going to gift shows to try and expand. I had met this businessman that told us that he wanted to distribute our products, wanted to take our business to the next level. I had trepidation about taking this next step. John Roger said, "It's OK for your business to get big; just don't get big with your business!" This reminder to keep my ego in check was so profound for me. It has affected my thinking for life. It doesn't matter if you have a big business or a small one, as long as you are a real, honest and caring person.

As time flowed on, my partner and I started doing wholesale trade shows. We set up and managed show rooms in gift markets all over the United States. At our peak, our sales were $10,000,000 at retail, selling products of rare beauty. We saw the crystals as being mechanisms of sparking loveliness. Our byline was the Gift of Light. Because of my spiritual background, I knew the word "light" had many different meanings. Embracing this opportunity to act as a purveyor of beauty and illumination, I was able to use all of my visionary and persuasive talents.

At BigSpeak it has been a challenge to move beyond booking experts for keynote addresses. Research shows that, with a keynote address, there is only about 5% retention of information three to six months down the road. That's not impressive. But consulting and training and coaching can bump information retention and behavior improvement to a much higher level. There is so much ground to cover, so many opportunities and organizational changes to address. Translating these opportunities into profit centers, while serving our customers, is important. As I keep an open mind, I know I will figure out the next steps for BigSpeak.

With an interesting and accomplished past behind me, I am looking towards the future. After almost 40 total years of doing business, I feel drawn to the next great thing. I've always been in sales or acted as an agent for others, for the talent. Now I'm wondering, is it time for me to be the talent, to write a book or lead workshops or do inspirational speaking? Or, is it time to do something completely new? The one thing I do know is that I will land on my feet!

I know that, with the help of others, I've created two successful companies supported by great teams that have had a huge impact. Today, I receive respect from top decision makers and am aware of the positive effect that has resulted from my professional efforts.

It's always a challenge to be the final decision maker in an organization. But I'm not a top-down kind of guy. I really seek a degree of consensus. I know it's healthy to hear what people know, what they think, even if their opinions are unfavorable. At Iris Arc, there was a woman that we could count on to bring up the most difficult things that employees were thinking but would never say. She challenged us, but that only made us a better company. So, one of my legacies is that, today, I am a leader who works to gain the buy-in of my team through encouraging their full participation in our decision making processes.

With all the success I have had, there is one unsung hero left in my life, one man that stood behind me for many years and led by example, from day one. Just thinking about him takes me back to my Southern California upbringing, back to moving and moving again, to new neighborhoods, new schools, new challenges.

My final mentor and hero is my dad. He wasn't a flashy guy. He worked in the defense industry as a project manager. He worked hard, he was diligent and made sure his projects came in on time and within budget. The quality I took from him was to be very consistent and very steady, to be someone others could trust and count on. He was never in the limelight and I don't know of any awards that he won. But, he showed up every day with the best of intentions and worked in a very practical way. He was good at taking care of his family. And, I grew up knowing he loved me, my sister and brother, and my mom.

Looking back, my father's legacy was solid and steadfast. My father's legacy was being honest and loving his family. He always put family first. And, he did a wonderful job. I trust that I am doing the same with my family with my loving intentions, actions and consistency. Life is good!

"I don't want to die the richest man
buried in the graveyard."

LARRY RUVO

Who is Larry Ruvo? Since 1969 Larry Ruvo has been
senior managing director of Southern Wine and Spirits
of Nevada, the state's largest wholesale liquor, wine and beer
importer and distributor. He is also well known in the Las Vegas
community for his ongoing support associated with education and
children. He was presented the Altruistic Award by the Meadows
School, a pre-K through 12 private school that he helped to
establish. As a trustee for the UNLV Foundation, Larry donates
all proceeds from annual wine tasting events (UNLVino) to
scholarship funds for the William F. Harrah College of Hotel
Administration students. Larry Ruvo is also a founding member
of the Young Presidents' Organization (YPO). Nevada chapter,
a former member of the World Presidents' Organization, bailli
of the Chaine des Rotisseurs in Las Vegas, and a member of
the Bluecoats in Nevada (an organization established to help
families of firemen and police officers killed in the line of
duty). He currently serves as a board member of the Nevada
Ballet Theatre and a board member of the American Gaming

Association (AGA). He is a founding member of the Nevada Tourism Alliance as well as the Council for a Better Nevada.

In 1994, after the loss of his father, Lou Ruvo, to Alzheimer's disease, Larry made it his mission to establish a cognitive disease center, which resulted in his founding the Keep Memory Alive Foundation, which funds the Cleveland Clinic Lou Ruvo Center for Brain Health. The center, housed in a building designed by internationally renowned architect Frank Gehry, has become the world's epicenter for research on neurodegenerative diseases such as Alzheimer's, Huntington's, Parkinson's, ALS and multiple sclerosis, and for caring for the patients, families and caregivers affected by these diseases.

Larry has also been the recipient of numerous honors. He was recognized as Man of the Year by MDA and received the 1999 Community Leadership Award from the Points of Light Foundation. In addition, he received Man of the Year awards from the University of Nevada Las Vegas, the Food & Beverage Directors Association, and numerous other charitable organizations. Larry received the UNLV President's Medal and is listed as one of the most Influential Businessmen of Southern Nevada for the years 2004 and 2009 and was also included as one of the Vegas Dozen in 2005. Larry was inducted into the 2005 Gaming Hall of Fame and honored by the Public Education Foundation with the Education Hero Award for 2005.

In July 2006, President George W. Bush appointed Larry to serve as a member of the prestigious Advisory Committee to the Arts at the John F. Kennedy Center for the Performing Arts. He was presented the Governor's Philanthropist of the Year Award. In 2007, the *Las Vegas Review Journal* named Larry Ruvo "Most Favorite Male in Las Vegas." In 2008 Larry was asked to serve as the Nevada co-chair for the George W. Bush Presidential Center, and continues to work on this historic project. In 2009, he was named Distinguished Nevadan by UNLV and was honored with the Woodrow Wilson Award in 2009.

Larry was also asked to join the board of trustees of the esteemed Cleveland Clinic in 2009. In May 2010 Larry received the Angel Awards 2010 Humanitarian of the Year from In Business. Larry also received the Nevada Business Hall of Fame award on February 7, 2013, and the Horatio Alger award for Distinguished Americans in April 2013.

Larry is married to Camille and has three daughters: Nicole, Lauren and Brianna.

For more information please visit **www.keepmemoryalive.org** and **www.my.clevelandclinic.org/neurological_institute/lou-ruvo-brain-health**.

•••

I grew up in Las Vegas, where my mom and dad owned the Venetian Restaurant. It was a tiny family business. I started working there at the age of seven, grating cheese, washing pots and pans, and making spumoni with my hands—the worst job because my hands always froze.

I worked at the restaurant until I was 14, and during those seven years I decided I knew everything there was to know about running the business. One Friday my father came in and said, "Did you fire Chef John Kirk?"

I said, "Yes Dad, but you don't understand what was going on."

"First thing that you need to know," he said, "you never fire a chef on a Friday afternoon. You've got to hire John back and then fire him on Monday."

So I grudgingly called John over to the table and hired him back.

"John," my father said, "Now that Larry has hired you back, I am promoting you to general manager . . . and your first job is to fire my son."

I never worked for my dad again, but that moment taught me so much. By making me re-hire John and then having him fire me instead of Dad just saying, "I'm firing you and I am hiring John back," my father taught me about business and respecting people.

He taught me a million other things, too many to list here, but one thing stands out: he stressed how important it was to try to avoid legal contracts as much as possible, to use handshakes wherever you can. I still believe in that. In the last 90 days alone I concluded three very big deals—one worth a million dollars—with not a single syllable in writing with an attorney. On that million dollar deal I said this was how we were going to do it, and that I trusted them. In this case I happened to be dealing with Emilio and Gloria Estefan. They're ethical people, so we just shook hands on it. If you can't get a deal done with a handshake, it might mean there's not enough trust in the situation to do the deal at all.

I also had other mentors that I admired, including a couple of world leaders. When I was a younger man I was moved by Gandhi. While I don't recommend that people go out and starve themselves, he liberated his country and changed the whole world by simply standing up to the British Empire—and he did so passively, without any fighting.

I've always had immense respect for President George H.W. Bush. I had the good fortune to spend some time with him in Kennebunkport. If you watch the documentary *41* you'll understand the man's intellect and experience, how he knew when he had to be number two (vice president to President Reagan) and how that differed from being number one. I also truly respected how much he loves his family.

Pope John Paul II—now Saint John Paul II—was another man I respect enormously. I had the good fortune of receiving Holy Communion from him, as did my daughter. This priest, then pope, and now saint, really changed the world—and did a lot of it through his work with the younger generations. During all his travels he knew his platform had to revolve around the young people to make a difference for our future generations.

I also learned from these men a sense of responsibility to others. From the very beginning, part of my business was to give back to that community. It started one day in the early 1970s when Steve Wynn and I were at the Young Presidents' Organizations (YPO) conference being held at Caesar's Palace. One of the speakers was a gentleman who at the time owned the Riviera Hotel and Casino—Meshulam Riklis. He was talking about what you needed to do to launch a business. One of the things he said was, "When you start your business you need to get involved with the community. You need the community to know who you are. You need to give back!"

Steve raised his hand and asked, "Well, how do you give back when you're starting a company and you're not even profitable?"

Riklis said, "You'd better figure out how to do it, because if you don't your competitors will. Give back—if not with money, then with product; if not with product, then with physical time. Whatever it is, you've got to get your company's name out there to the community, to the people who will eventually support you."

From that point on Steve and I did, and still do, an enormous amount of charitable work. In fact my involvement in the community has risen to a higher level because what I do influences my employees. If you think about it charitable work can be self-perpetuating. Southern Wine and Spirits of Nevada has 750 people. If they see me doing something for the community and just 10% of them join in, that's 75 people doing something. If their spouses join that's another 75—and if they have kids . . . well, all of a sudden there's a groundswell of giving back. I'm convinced that even if we cannot change the world, we can change our city. And that's what we've tried to do daily at Southern Wine and Spirits of Nevada.

Of course, while they are not world leaders, I owe a huge debt to my parents. My father always had the philosophy that you never loan money to family, you give it to them. For one thing, chances are they will never pay you back, and if you expect them to, you create an enemy. So if you can't afford to give money to a family member, or you know they won't be able to pay you back, you might not want to loan them anything. My father felt it was better to just help them out if they were in need.

My mother, on the other hand, gave money to whomever asked, even when we didn't have any money. There's an infamous story about when our family lived in a 900 square foot house on Beverly Way. Two bedrooms, one bath; you could hear through the walls. One day my parents were in the kitchen arguing. They hardly ever argued, but that day they were really going at it. At the time construction was underway on St. Anne's Catholic Church on Maryland Parkway. My mom had come home and said she'd made a pledge toward the construction fund for the church—a pledge for what was a lot of money at that time.

My father was beside himself. "How could you possibly make a donation? We don't even have any money to pay the rent!"

"God will take care of us," Mom replied.

The argument went on and on and on; I could hear it from my bedroom.

"Look," my mom said. "I signed the pledge card. God will take care of us. Don't worry about it!" And that was the end of the argument.

Well, God did take care of them. Today if you walk into St. Anne's Church you'll see a plaque reading "Mr. and Mrs. Louis Ruvo." When I see it I remember how it got there: through personal sacrifice. It got there because a woman wrote out a pledge card even when she didn't have any money to back it up. She said she would do it, and she did. Obviously, despite the argument, my dad supported her decision.

My parents' understanding of generosity went beyond family and faith, however. I was an only child, so the three of us would discuss a lot of things around our dinner table. During one of those discussions my father told me, "One day, if you ever become wealthy, remember that you can only eat one steak and drive one Cadillac, and after you have your house paid off, the rest of the money should go to the less fortunate."

We never did get rich, but I don't eat steak and I don't drive a Cadillac and God has been good to me.

My dad's philosophy and the way I was brought up was with the feeling that I don't want to die the richest man buried in the graveyard. I'd rather support the less fortunate than die with a large bank account.

I remember when Ted Turner, a very controversial guy, was ranked in the Forbes 500. He'd just given away billions of dollars, and people told him, "You know, Mr. Turner, this might take you off of the Forbes 500." He said, "It's only a number. It doesn't matter if I'm zero or 500. Who cares?"

Over the years, I've learned it's an unbelievable feeling to change people's lives. I've walked through the Cleveland Clinic Lou Ruvo Brain Center for Brain Health and looked at the faces of the patients and their families and had people come up to touch me and thank me. Now, do I feel better with having this facility, or with a bank statement that says I made more money this month than last month? The answer is obvious when I walk through that building and see the people we are helping.

Of course, I can't walk through the center without thinking of what started it all. When my father got sick I went around for a year watching him get these God-awful tests and spinal taps in Las Vegas. Finally I took him to the experts, and they immediately found out the diagnosis: Alzheimer's. But that year of agony I don't forget; the level of incompetence I don't forget; nor have I forgotten that after I buried my dad I had to take my mother in for surgery. We had been ignorant of what a caregiver goes through; how they are sleep deprived and stressed out and often die before the patient they're taking care of.

Now, my mom has always been a big part of my life. She's 90 years old and has been there for me every step of the way despite the long, hard road I have traveled to build a profitable business and establish my place in the Las Vegas community. Her devotion to my father and how she suffered as a result was at the core of what I wanted to do for caregivers.

More than anything, I didn't want any of those things to happen to my friends and family again. I wanted people to know that caregivers are very hard-working, respectful people, and that they do an amazing, remarkable, unbelievable job. So I decided to tell my father's story. ... But over time, simply telling the story evolved into constructing a building on my father's behalf. And not just any building—I wanted a structure that would let people know how serious I was. It was designed by the celebrity architect Frank Gehry and cost over $100 million. I wanted people to think, "Whoa, this guy must be serious!"

I then partnered with the Cleveland Clinic and some of the world's greatest minds in neurology, and as the center evolved we brought an enormous amount of talent to Las Vegas. For me, the cherry on top was when the Cleveland Clinic with its 47,000 employees and 3,000 doctors renamed their clinics in Florida and Ohio to the Cleveland Clinic Lou Ruvo Center for Brain Health, and adopted my policy of having no patient waiting rooms and of taking care of the caregiver.

It's a remarkable feeling to help people. If everybody in the world would just help one other person, imagine the possibilities of what this world would be like.

It bears repeating: Who cares if you die the richest guy in the graveyard? I believe you have to take care of your children's essentials and whatever else you need to do, but the rest of your money? I think you would feel better using it to help other people...At least I do!

The Legacy of
JUSTICE

*"Justice will not be served until those who are unaffected
are as outraged as those who are."*
— Benjamin Franklin

Examples of injustice bombard us daily. We need merely turn on the television or surf the Internet to see news stories about innocent lives lost or ravaged by war, corrupt government leaders who enrich themselves while their people suffer, and children abandoned or abused by a broken system of bureaucratic mismanagement, to name just a few. Most of us are forced to sit idly by and shake our heads, wondering "How can this be? Why doesn't someone do something about this?" We then put aside those unpleasant images and go about our busy lives.

But to some, bearing witness to or suffering the pain of injustice is a life-changing experience, a call to action that might ignite the fire of a passion that burns throughout their lives. These are the people whose devotion to their cause may change the perceptions of justice that others have, and perhaps even alter the future.

*"Assisting families whose lives have been devastated
or destroyed at the hands of an impaired driver
leaves an inconsolable ache in your heart."*

SANDY HEVERLY

Who is Sandy Heverly? Sandy Heverly is the executive director and co-founder of Stop DUI, a Nevada grassroots nonprofit organization dedicated to stopping the violent crime of driving under the influence (DUI) and assisting the victims of this crime.

Ms. Heverly's involvement with the anti-DUI movement began in Las Vegas, Nevada, in 1983, when virtually all of her family was seriously injured by a drunk driver. The offender was underage, had two prior DUIs, was driving on a suspended license, speeding, ran a stop sign and left the scene—and received a $100 fine for his crimes.

Sandy quickly learned that driving under the influence was not viewed as a serious or violent crime by the public in general and the judiciary in particular. As a result she established a Victim's Assistance Program that includes immediate financial assistance to needy DUI victims. Stop DUI is the only anti-DUI organization in the country that provides that level of assistance.

Recognizing the importance of education and awareness of the crime of driving under the influence, Ms. Heverly founded and coordinates a speaker's bureau that presents to schools, civic organizations, businesses, prisons and juvenile offender facilities. Believing that DUI offenders should see and hear firsthand the devastation caused to victims, Sandy also created the first DUI Victim Impact Panel concept in the nation.

Ms. Heverly's legislative efforts include the passage of laws to benefit the innocent victims of crime in general and DUI victims in particular, and promoting the anti-DUI message in all kinds of media. She has sat on numerous boards and committees to address crime victim rights and DUI issues, and in 2003 coordinated a coalition to defeat the attempts of the Marijuana Policy Project to legalize three ounces of marijuana in the state of Nevada. Her tireless efforts contributed to the Marijuana Ballot Initiative being defeated 61% to 39%.

Among numerous other awards and presentations, Ms. Heverly was honored by President George Bush, US Attorney General Richard Thornberg and the US Department of Justice in a Rose Garden Ceremony for her outstanding contributions regarding victim's rights and DUI legislation. She was selected from among 200 individuals from around the nation to receive this award, the most prestigious in the victim's rights arena.

For more information please visit **www.stopdui.org**.

•••

I grew up in the outskirts of Chicago and lived in the Chicago area for a number of years before we moved to a little suburb called Park Forrest. That's where I went to school, made friends, and learned how to connect with people. In 1964, we moved to Nevada, where I met my biological father for the first time. To say the least, that was interesting. Very interesting . . .

This was also where I met my hero, a real life hero to me, who influenced every aspect of my life. He was visiting his brother, who lived next door to my father's home. Eventually, we married. Our marriage lasted for 49 years, three months and 26 days . . .

Precious time with my hero.

During that time I had no career. My life was focused on making a comfortable and loving home for our family. Having been raised in an Italian family, to me *familia* was always given precedence over anything else.

We had four children: two sons and two daughters. All were doing fine until the day before Father's Day in 1983, when we decided to take a road trip to Disneyland.

My husband was a blackjack dealer. He had a habit of playing keno, and that Saturday he'd won 1,200 dollars. Because of the extra money he was excited and wanted to celebrate. Having been raised an orphan from the age of two, he valued family above all else. When we married, my mother told him that she would be the mother he'd never had. So, on this exciting day, he asked me to call mom and invite her to share the fun with us.

She agreed. We spent the rest of the day preparing for the trip, packing all the games, snacks, pillows . . . everything to keep the children comfortable and occupied during the drive. I had my husband's Father's Day gifts in the back of the camper, too.

So we picked up Mom on our way to Disneyland. Everyone was happy, relaxed, as carefree as only a family going on a special outing can be. We drove to the intersection of Sandhill and Flamingo, and continued to the next cross street—Pearl.

That was when a car going 65 miles an hour in a 25 mile an hour zone ran through a stop sign and crashed into our truck and small camper. The truck and camper went into a spin so hard the bodies of my four children were blown out the back of the camper.

The driver was named Miles Barry Lefler. He had two prior DUIs and was driving under a suspended license—and not only was he drunk, he fled the scene like a coward.

The bodies of my children were scattered onto the roadway. My oldest son suffered numerous broken bones and internal injuries. My ten-year-old daughter had broken toes, a broken right hand and right arm. My eight-year-old son was literally skinned alive, his flesh left raw and bleeding after the skin was scraped off. My precious little two-and-a-half-year-old baby had a very serious concussion, all of her teeth knocked out and half of her chin ripped off her face. My husband's head was split open from the front to his neck. My head was cracked open in two places, my right hand and arm broken, all my ribs were on the right side broken, and I was blinded in my left eye and paralyzed on my left side.

But, my mom, my dear mom, got the worst of it. Her arm was almost completely severed and she was thrown beneath the truck. The engine fell and crushed her chest, then the truck caught fire and she was burned alive.

This was the scene—seven people, a once whole and healthy family, destroyed in a moment by one drunk driver.

It was a long time before we were physically able to go to court. Meanwhile, my mom spent three months in the burn unit. My children suffered post-traumatic stress disorder. After several months my husband tried to force himself back to work. We almost lost our home, and we discovered to our sadness and pain that there was nothing in place to protect DUI victims. Drunk driving simply wasn't viewed as a serious crime. It was just an "accident." Drunk driving was considered a joke. It *was* a joke. So when we finally got to court, there were no charges filed against Lefler. He received a $100 fine and walked out of the courtroom, laughing.

That was my introduction to the criminal justice system. It was like being arrested in a foreign country and, unable to speak the language, finding that no one cared about your imprisonment. All the lawyers and judges wanted to do was clear their dockets for the next case.

I decided to learn their language.

My mom spent months, weeks, endless days undergoing surgeries and rehabilitation, trying to recover from a multitude of injuries. She fought every physical and emotional assault with fortitude and dignity, but medical problems continued to develop and she died . . . the inscription on her gravestone reads: "A drinking driver changed my life."

As time passed I realized there was nothing going on when it came to either victim support or holding perpetrators accountable. Then, one day in October of 1982, my husband brought home a free magazine that contained an article about drunk driving. I thought, "Wow! I've got to contact these people to see what can be done to inform the public." What I really wanted was education for officers, legislators, and voters to teach them that drunk driving was truly a violent crime. At that time we were functioning under a national organization, and started a local chapter. My husband was very supportive. He never wanted to be in front of the camera or get glory, but he built shelves all over my office and hauled stuff from one place to another for events. And he never, ever complained about the demands of his contribution, or my hours. All this while he was working two jobs so I could do whatever I needed to do. He worked these two jobs for nearly eight years, then had a heart attack.

During these months I was still naïve to the flaws in the legal system. I was ignorant of the games that were played. But I learned quickly. Unfortunately, many officers and judges drove while under the influence, which limited their desire to apply retribution. There but for the grace of God . . . they thought. Such attitudes had been ingrained for many years. It's hard to move a mountain. . . .

During this struggle my husband, John, gave me unconditional love and support for what I was doing—not only for me, his wife, but for my mission. "Don't worry about anything else," he said. "Just concentrate on what you have to do. I'll be here for you."

You think that when something so horrible happens you'll grow a thicker skin, develop immunity. But that's not true. I know firsthand, because later, *another* drunk driver came crashing through a stop sign and injured me and my sister. Mrs. Shirley Jean Schaffer, with a blood alcohol content of .28, was on her way to a baby shower and oblivious of the stop sign.

At this time, DUI victims—all crime victims, really—had no legal right to speak at sentencing. Rectifying this inequity became a priority for me. I feel blessed to have participated in creating a statute that assures the voice of the victim is heard.

Some of this process was overwhelming, especially when dealing with death and injury cases on a daily basis. Multiple victims are especially challenging when family dynamics come into play. Assisting families whose lives have been devastated or destroyed at the hands of an impaired driver leaves an inconsolable ache in your heart.

I'm blessed to have many people working with me. When doing an event, we have close to 100 dedicated volunteers involved. We can count on two to three thousand documented supporters, and community support is astounding. It's heartwarming to know that the majority of people do care, and all of us have the same goal . . . eradicating DUI and saving lives . . . that's why we founded Stop DUI. I've had the honor and privilege of functioning as the executive director and victim advocate for this organization for 20 years, and can say without reservation that the people in this group are the best of the best.

I've also encountered many wonderful mentors during this journey. For example, Florence McClure, who founded the Rape Crisis Center. I met her at a meeting of the Citizen's Coalition for Victim's Rights, which Governor Bob Miller founded 35 years ago. I was awestruck by Florence's tenacity and concern for crime victims. She took me under her wing and encouraged me to never give up and always stay focused on the mission. She knew the ropes like no other. Her guidance in terms of getting established and going about things in a certain way to get desired results, combined with her belief in my ability to make a difference, contributed greatly to my sustaining the mission for the last 31 years.

My most satisfying contributions were the ones others helped me achieve. It was always extremely disturbing during a sentencing to hear the judge read all the defendant's rights, including the right to address the court, but offer nothing on behalf of the victim. How could a judge impose an appropriate sentence without seeing the full picture? DUI victim Vern Lewton and I requested that former State Assembly Judiciary Chairman Robert Sader sponsor legislation that would grant all crime victims the right to give an oral victim impact statement at the time of sentencing. Finally, the voice of the victim would be heard.

Equally disturbing was the fact that DUI victims did not qualify to receive financial aid from the State Victims of Crime Compensation Office. The excuse was that DUI victims would deplete the fund! This was utter nonsense, and I presented the research to the legislature to prove it.

I sought assistance and support from then lieutenant governor Bob Miller. He joined me in testifying in support of that legislation, after which DUI victims became classified as "crime victims," allowing them to receive assistance from the Victims of Crime Compensation Fund. This piece of legislation also assisted with educating legislators, judges, and law enforcement to the fact DUI was not only a serious crime, but a violent crime as well.

Educating the public to this fact and to the alternatives to driving under the influence required a major attitude change. When we began this mission, 67% of all traffic fatalities were alcohol-related. Nowadays the average is between 30%–32%—a significant accomplishment, although of no consolation to those who continue to be victimized by impaired drivers.

One of our most successful programs is the Stop DUI Victim Impact Panel. The concept originated here and has been recognized at the local, state and national level. I believed if misdemeanor DUI offenders could see and hear firsthand from DUI victims the kind of damage they could be responsible for causing, it would help change their behavior. And it has! Our Victim Impact Panels have a 92% success rate in reducing recidivism.

Offenders pay a fee to attend the 90 minute program, and those funds help provide the most extensive DUI victim assistance program in the country. We are the only anti-DUI organization that provides immediate and direct financial assistance to needy, innocent DUI victims, and we're very proud of that. These funds also allow us to provide specialized law enforcement DUI training, DUI equipment, and education and awareness programs.

We work with the most amazing and courageous people... people who have been brought to us under the most horrific circumstances and are willing to stand before an audience of DUI offenders to relive the most heart-wrenching and painful experience of their lives. They give of their time and hearts with the hope of changing at least one person's behavior.

One thing I learned very quickly was that even though the circumstances might be different in each case, the senseless pain, suffering, grief and sorrow of DUI victims are universal. All crime victims need guidance through the judicial system, as well as caring support for however long the grieving and recovery process takes. DUI victims are not just case numbers. You get to know them personally, a bond develops, and they become part of a very special extended family.

If our efforts help prevent this type of pain and suffering from happening to other families, then that's the icing on the cake...

I'm often asked, "Why do you do what you do?" Well, for very selfish reasons. I'm trying to protect what I have left, and not have my family victimized by another drunk driver. Staying focused on the mission is important to achieving the goal, and never forgetting that there is no immunity to this crime. Drunk drivers don't discriminate and they never take a day off.

And one person can make a difference—for good or ill. Larry Mahoney was responsible for creating the worst drunk driving crash in the history of the United States when he drove drunk down the wrong side of a Kentucky freeway and smashed into a school bus. The bus exploded into flames. Twenty-four children and three adults burned to death, and 34 other children were severely burned and injured. Yes, one person really can make a difference!

I've also learned that being a DUI victim advocate is a 24/7 responsibility. Drunk drivers don't limit their destruction to between the hours of nine and five. And DUI victims might need help and or a listening ear at any hour of the day or night.

This is where my soul mate of 49 years, three months and 26 days, my personal hero, John, comes into the picture yet again.

Whenever I had to respond to a crisis situation he would always say, "Just be careful, honey," and "Do what you have to do, beautiful blue eyes." And that was it! Never a complaint about how long I would be gone, or the numerous phone calls and media visits to our home, or the time spent in court, at the office and special events. I was blessed with that extraordinary level of support that allowed me to stay focused on the goal. I've worked with many great volunteers who don't have that support and struggle with the personal demands some family members inflict upon them.

John contributed so very much with his loving, quiet, encouraging, behind the scenes support. He was a great sounding board for my speeches and never hesitated to give me his honest opinion if I was missing the mark. I was the one in front of the camera while he did all the hard work without praise or fanfare.

He had the patience of a saint...something I don't have!

That's how it was for all those years up until the day he died. Since he's been gone, I constantly ask myself what he would want me to do. I don't believe he'd want me to curl up in a ball and isolate myself...although, truthfully, at times, that's exactly what I feel like doing. But then I hear his voice saying, "Do what you have to do, beautiful blue eyes." So I will—because to do less would dishonor all the selfless sacrifices he made.

"These kids were in a very bad situation themselves, but were willing to help other human beings."

MICHAEL AND

ESTHER BROWN

Who are Michael and Esther Brown? Together, husband and wife Michael Brown and Esther Brown run a nonprofit organization called the Embracing Project. The project's mission is to promote peace and global consciousness through the development programs they conduct to enrich the lives of children, youth, and families all over the world.

Michael Brown played professional basketball with the Harlem Globetrotters and for 11 years in the NBA with teams such as the Phoenix Suns, Philadelphia 76ers, Minnesota Timberwolves, Utah Jazz and Chicago Bulls. He was the former head coach in the NBA Developmental League, and assistant coach of the Chicago Bulls. He was inducted into the George Washington University Hall of Fame and recognized as Man of the Year by the Salt Lake City Boys and Girls Club.

Esther Brown, born and raised in Barcelona, Spain, was always concerned with and involved in social issues. She volunteered in an adult prison where she helped inmates and other nonprofit organizations, and founded the Embracing Project in 2005. She was nominated for the 2013 Peace Progress Award, 2013 L'Oreal Woman of Worth, and 2013 El-Hibri Peace Education Prize.

For more information please visit **www.theembracingproject. org**.

•••

Michael's Story. I was an only child born in Newark, New Jersey. My belief is that everything kind of begins at home. Regardless of where we lived—in the projects, in the house, wherever it was—my home was my foundation. There were rules. I respected them and had to work hard in school I couldn't go out and do things unless I got good grades and did my homework.

My mother and grandmother were my inspiration. My mom's name was Roselee—Rose—and she sacrificed tremendously just to raise me. I was a big kid who ate a lot and was constantly growing out of clothes and shoes. My pants were always high-water even though she was constantly buying me new clothes. She sewed her own clothes because that type of money wasn't coming in. Mom was a hard worker, yet she also did a lot of giving back to the community. For example, she got involved in Junior Achievement to teach young people the business side of the world, and gave sewing classes to young ladies.

She put me in a private Catholic school and worked bingo as part of her stipend for the reduced tuition on my behalf. She stressed the importance of education, especially on the math side. When I was five or six years old she worked at a bank, then went on to work in another company in the accounting department. She enforced that you needed math to survive in the world. Math and science are the tougher subjects and we have a tendency to go away from them instead of applying ourselves. Education is the key to escaping from the ghetto.

She was big on having kids come over to our house versus me going over to theirs; that way she could look into the backyard and see what we were doing. Of course, kids wanted to come over to our place because my mother always had food available. Also, most of those kids really couldn't talk to their parents, but with my mom you could bring up any topic. She'd tell you what she thought about it, and then tell you what to do.

During the summer I stayed with my grandmother, Jessie Mae—nicknamed Saf. She was a cheerful and happy-go-lucky woman, but also someone you didn't want to mess with. Everyone in the neighborhood respected her.

Let me illustrate. When I was growing up in the projects there were quite a few break-ins, especially at the beginning of the month after people got their government assistance checks and went out and bought the things they needed. We all knew the one or two families that were doing the breaking in, but because we all had to go on living there nobody ever called the cops on them. Our neighbors on the right and left got hit over more than once, but never our place. Saf said, "They haven't broken into my house because they respect me."

She was one to yell out the window when a kid was misbehaving: "I'm going to tell your mother and father about what you're doing!" That was what I learned growing up: if you treat people fairly and honestly, the goodness in them will come out.

When I first starting playing ball as a kid, I spent a lot of time at the Boys and Girls Club in Newark's Central Ward. The Boys and Girls Club kept me off the streets. I was there every day in the summer and I was a member of the ping-pong, chess, gym, basketball, track and billiards teams. That was the best three dollars a month I ever spent. Thank you Mr. Rudy, club director. After winning the state basketball championship in high school, I got a scholarship to play at George Washington University, and graduated with a degree in criminal justice in three and a half years. In 1985 I got drafted to the Chicago Bulls, and for the next 16 years played professional basketball. Eleven of those years were in the NBA and five were overseas—three in Italy and two in Spain. For four years I coached in the NBA D-League, then returned to the Bulls as an assistant coach in 2007.

I never forgot the importance the Boys and Girls Clubs had in my life. As a professional, when I traveled to different cities to play I always visited different Boys and Girls Clubs to help provide kids with a male role model and contribute to a positive atmosphere. I would give T-shirts to camps and just spend time with them. In 1989 the Salt Lake City Boys and Girls Club presented me with a plaque for Man of the Year. That was an incredible honor and it still hangs on my wall today.

I left the Bulls in 2008 in order to work with our organization, the Embracing Project, which my wife had started while I was coaching in the D-League. It was entirely Esther's brainchild; she envisioned the project and developed the curriculum and the website, and decided we were going to focus on helping kids globally.

The Embracing Project gave me a global perspective on giving. I already knew what was needed in the inner cities in America, but now, from a global standpoint, I could see that there were children far worse off than they were here. My response was inspired by the kind of giving I remembered from my mother and grandmother. Back in the day, if you had a pot of stew you shared it with a neighbor and their kids.

The most influential people in my life were my mother, grandmother and my mom's brother. My mother would give my old clothes to families and feed whomever needed a meal. Saf would tell me the story that she used to breast-feed other children when their mothers were low on milk. Now that's feeding the neighborhood!

Saf was big on Sunday family dinner. My mom, uncle Buddy and me. I remember one Sunday Uncle Buddy was more than an hour late. When he arrived, he had a story to tell. He was sitting at a red light, the door was unlocked, and a man jumped into the passenger seat. He was holding his side and bleeding. He asked if my uncle could take him to the hospital—and he did. I believe that if you help one person a week, the world would be a better place.

I wanted to share what I'd learned growing up in Newark in a single-parent household. I understand what it's like not having much money, or when your parents are sacrificing to provide for you, so I can relate to the kids. For example, I know how poverty affects schooling. It's hard to have kids sit there for two hours trying to learn something when they're hungry. You cannot have that. I understand their situation, and it helps me get the kids to open up because they know I relate to where they're coming from.

Another helpful angle is the sports. The boys and girls enjoy basketball, and they love the NBA. Although they didn't see me play, the teams I played for are still there and the kids relate to them.

It takes time before it starts showing results. At first you're just trying to provide, trying to educate. You don't know how to fix the kids because they don't tell you how they feel right away. After a class you might get a letter or a kid might pull you aside and tell you how great the experience was, and you hear things from the parents or see changes in the kids' activities. It's very rewarding when you hear about a success; that's the fuel that keeps you going, because sometimes it's tough. Even if your efforts work for three kids out of four, you focus on the one failure and ask yourself what you're doing wrong.

You want to save them all, and the irony is that you can't. The best way to look at it is to think, "If I can help one kid it will create a snowball affect and trickle down, because that one changed life will affect everyone around him or her, and also his or her children some day."

Which is, come to think of it, exactly the kind of giving I learned from my mother, uncle and grandmother.

•••

Esther's Story. I was born and raised in Barcelona, Spain, but when I was seven my parents moved us to a very small town called Massanet de la Selva in the north of Spain, close to the French border.

In school I was not the best student. Although I love to read and I question everything, I wasn't very good at following rules, so I got into enough trouble that I had to repeat high school several times. Now I joke with the kids I work with that it's never too late to start over, because I was almost 20 before I graduated from high school.

After that I decided to go to law school...but two weeks before classes began I got married. Law school was my honeymoon.

My marriage was not good but I have an amazing daughter that was born as a result of that relationship. After almost three years attending law school I decided to change and start psychology school; I felt that law looks good in the books but sometimes is not applied fairly. I didn't finish studying psychology, either. No wonder my family used to say, "Esther always starts things and never finishes."

Then, in February of 2000, I met Mike Brown in Barcelona, I did not speak English at the time and Mike did not speak Spanish, but we both speak Italian; that is how we communicated for the first years in our relationship. I came for the first time to visit Las Vegas in July 2000, but I wasn't moving to another country with my daughter without knowing Mike well. During that visit I met Mike's children and we strengthened our relationship, but it still was to premature for me to join him in the US. So he turned down a job in Sacramento to accept one in Orense (Spain) so we could be together in my country first to see if our relationship was strong. We lived in Orense until April 2001 and by the end of that month we decided to move to Las Vegas.

Moving to Las Vegas was a cultural shock. I didn't speak English very well, but it wasn't just that. The culture, the family union, is different here. And we were living in Las Vegas, which is a special place. People don't talk to each other there as we do in Spain. If you go to a restaurant and say, "hi," people look at you like, "Why you are saying Hi to me? I don't know you." So it was very hard for me my first two years. In addition, I did not have any family members here for support. It was difficult for me, but it was also hard for my daughter Andrea; she was six years old at the time and she had to go through the same process of adaptation.

I told Mike I wanted to learn English, go to college and get a degree, and I did. In 2009 I graduated with honors in criminal justice from the University of Phoenix. At that time we were living in North Carolina, where Mike was coaching a minor league NBA team. I started volunteering in a detention center in Fayetteville teaching Spanish; at the same time it was a good exposure to learn how the juvenile justice system works.

What I discovered at the detention center was a revolving door: the same kids commonly came back and left, came back and left, time and again. So in one of my classes I asked them about it. "Obviously the food here is not good," I said, "and the uniform is not very stylish, so what's the attraction?"

They told me they had no place to go on the outside. After being released they were dropped right back in the same environment they'd left, with the same people and the same situations.

In the United States the largest group of immigrants is Latino. In Spain it's Africans, particularly from central and northern Africa. While living in Spain I'd been involved with African groups and had African friends; in fact, ever since I was a little kid I'd wanted to visit Africa. Maybe in a past life I was African; all I know is that I always had an attraction to African culture.

One day rather than teach Spanish I decided to show the kids in the detention center about the reality of certain countries; in Africa, especially about child soldiers. It seemed to me that a lot of our kids here are soldiers, too; they're born into violence and have to survive in the streets, so that's how they communicate—through violence. So I explained them the situation of and stories of the child soldiers in Uganda. The kids were overwhelmed. "Wow, what can we do? Can we help them? Can you bring them here? Can we go there?" I was amazed. These kids were in a very bad situation themselves, but they were willing to help other human beings. I thought I could work with that desire to help, I think that the hope to help others become the hope to help themselves.

That made me realize there is goodness inside of everybody. Why we are so ready to focus on the bad things that these kids do? Why don't we focus on developing the humanitarian side that everybody has inside themselves?

I came back home and talked to my husband. "I know I want to do something," I said. "I have to do something about this." He thought I was crazy. He pointed out that my English wasn't too good at the time; what did I think I was going to do?

I started researching gangs. The more I looked into the situation the more it reminded me of the genocides going on in parts of Africa, or those that had happened in Europe such as Bosnia, including the Nazi genocide of the Jews. Here we had a group of people—street gangs, including children—who were targeting different groups just because they hated what the other group represented. If I'm *Surenos*, I hate what *Nortenos* represent. I hate your colors, I hate your neighborhood, and I hate *you* because you're something that I am not. *Surenos* and *Nortenos*, Bloods and Crips—they hate each other because that's what they're taught to do: hate each other's guts.

According to the United Nations, genocide within a country can be recognized by eight characteristics: First, *classification*: we are divided. Second, *symbolization*: these symbols and colors differentiate us from other groups and represent hate against the other group. Third, *dehumanization*: we believe our enemies are not human. Fourth, *organization:* the group is organized, trained, and armed. Fifth, *polarization:* the protection of the leaders. Sixth, *identification:* people are identified prior to be harmed, there is a "fake" belief that gangs kill random people but the majority of time there is a previous identification, they had some type of previous conflict before they are targeted. Seventh, *extermination:* we will wipe out our enemies. And finally, eighth, *denial:* we justify our actions by various means so as to not feel bad about what we have done.

It occurred to me that gangs do exactly the same thing. The kids say, "I have to shoot them before they shoot me." Or, "He killed my homie, so it's okay for me to kill him." But they don't confront the reality of their actions.

That's why I think of what's happening in this country as a silent genocide. Nobody wants to talk about it because we live in the USA and the kids being killed are viewed as throwaways, but they deserve to be given the opportunity to understand their situation and be empowered to change it. Based on what I learned, when I came back to Las Vegas I put on a 12-week curriculum to teach the similarities between gangs and genocide and I started teaching the curriculum at Summit View, a maximum-security facility for juveniles. We called the curriculum "Healing the World Together." It taught kids about nonviolence and gratitude, about empathy and talking to other human beings. It taught life skills—the most simple things, like introducing yourself and how to listen to another person. Summit View closed in 2009, so now I lead similar groups in the Juvenile Detention Center and the Clark County Detention Center in Nevada, focusing on children who are being sent into the adult system. In Nevada we still do that—we treat kids who commit certain crimes as adults.

I wanted to work with child soldiers in Africa, but when I came to Las Vegas I realized the problems were similar here. The more I spoke to the kids the more I saw them as child soldiers being recruited by older gangsters to do their dirty work. Or sometimes the kids are *born* into a gang. After all, if my entire family—father, mother, cousins, uncles—are members of a gang, what are the chances of me doing something different?

I called the United Nations' office and I told them I wanted to create a pen pal program between former child soldiers and youths in gangs. I also wanted to take children from here that were involved in the juvenile system over to a country in Africa to do humanitarian work so they could see firsthand the consequences and the effects. Perhaps the pain that they shared could help heal the other.

I was told that at that time Sierra Leone was on the map because of the movie *Blood Diamond* and Uganda because of the Invisible Children documentary. People knew about countries like Uganda and Sierra Leone, but they didn't know too much about Liberia, a very small country of a little over four million that has gone through twenty years of bloody civil war. People don't know about Liberia. No one has done a movie about it.

I contacted a person there. He told me he loved my idea and asked me to come and visit them. So in 2008 I told my husband I was going to Liberia to see what was going on. Again, he said I was crazy. "The war only ended a couple of years before, why do you want to go *there?*" I said had to see, I needed to learn about it. So I went with a friend of mine and spent 15 days in Liberia.

We had bucket showers and cockroaches crawling onto our faces, we slept on the floor, and we really melded with the culture. I went to visit an orphanage in Bomy County and fell in love with the people and the kids. I met former child soldiers who were trying to come back without being judged by the community. They had performed atrocities because they were forced to. I thought, *Wow, this is amazing.* I wanted our gang kids to see how these kids had the courage to overcome lives of such poverty and violence.

So in 2009 I took a group of girls who were coming out of very challenging situations to Liberia. The result was amazing, it was a miracle! The girls, ages 15 to 17, worked in orphanages; they worked with former child soldiers; they worked with girls who had been sex slaves during the civil war; they met the vice president of Liberia and they shared their stories with them. They all thought it was a life-changing event.

By now I've spoken to thousands of kids, not only in detention centers but also at schools in Nevada and from California. We've also established a scholarship program in Liberia that's putting all the kids in Temas Orphanage through school. Next we plan to rehabilitate orphanages that have really bad conditions. We'd also like to bring more American youths to Liberia, but that's very expensive—about $8,000 dollars each because I don't put them through bucket showers; that would be too much. Unfortunately staying in a hotel is very expensive. There is no running water or central electricity in Liberia; everything is powered by generator.

But we do what we can. Our mission is to promote peace and higher consciousness, especially amongst people caught up in violence. It makes a difference when you find out you have a choice. When you allow people to become critical thinkers, they find the solutions within themselves. Otherwise they become like robots, just doing what they are told to do.

Since I was a child I've been moved by Gandhi and the way he freed his people in such a peaceful way, and how preached nonviolence. At the same time he showed the importance of keeping your dignity and not allowing people to step on you. The fact that you are nonviolent doesn't mean you are not a fighter—those are two different things—but you don't have to fight using violence, you can fight using other qualities like love and understanding.

I've always have been inspired by people who fight without weapons. Nelson Mandela was another of my heroes. When I was a teenager there was a TV show in my country where you could write and get the chance to meet your favorite singer or actor. I told my mother that I wanted to meet Nelson Mandela. She was, like, *OK*....

Now my heroes are the kids I work with. Every day I go to jail and talk to kids caught up in gangs and girls coming out of sex trafficking—they are the real heroes; they are the ones who keep me going. They're so resilient. You see on TV that one kid shot another kid, and you think, *Wow, that boy is bad, he's only 15 and he killed someone else!* But we have to ask: Why was he carrying a weapon at the age of 15 in the first place? Well, so he could feel safe in his own neighborhood. So when I sit and talk with these kids and they say, "Ah, miss, don't worry, I'll be OK," I see those as very strong people.

It's the same with the girls who went through sex trafficking or prostitution. Nobody wakes up one day and says, "I want to be a prostitute." They talk about how their fathers or cousins started touching them when they were four years old. They talk about growing up in abusive homes or foster homes. They talk about having a boyfriend who's 30 years old and promises to take them out of the situation they're in, so they sell their bodies out of love!

The first kid I ever put through my program was killed at the age of 19. He came to the Embracing Project when he was 15. Even though the youth complete the program we keep in touch with them forever and remain involved in their lives. That event was very hard for me. After him came others and you think it will get easy, but is never easy when a child or a young person dies because of violence and intolerance. When you try to change the world it's tempting to take on yourself the failures of others, but you can't—just as you can't take on their successes. I had to learn that I'm not here to save anyone; I'm just here to guide them. I'm here to share with them. To teach them that if you don't want to live this life anymore, if you want to do something different, you have to do it yourself. If you want to change the world that you live in, you have to change yourself first, and that is a personal task that no one can do for you.

At the same time I understand how difficult it is to change habits. Think about every New Year's Eve; you think, *I'm going to start that new diet and stop smoking*, and then January second comes around and you think, *Ah, whatever.* For these kids it's the same thing. They grow up in an environment of violence, so it's not easy for them to change. Even kids that we've worked with until the end—sometimes they try to get up, but for whatever reason they cannot; they get arrested. That's a part of the process. I tell them, "No matter how many times you fall, I will be there with you."

Some of them fall and never stand up again; they end up in prison or dead. Others have been very successful. We had one kid who now owns his own carpet cleaning business; we have kids who went on to college; we have kids who had no real parents of their own but are now great parents themselves.

Perhaps is difficult to have a world of peace and a world where unconditional love and respect for each other is our main belief, but difficult doesn't mean impossible.

"That is history, we can never change it . . .
but we are responsible for the future."

STEVEN NASSER

Who is Steven Nasser? Steven "Pista" Nasser was thirteen years old when the Nazis whisked him and his family away from their home in Hungary to Auschwitz. His memories of that terrifying experience are still vivid, and his love for his brother, Andris, still brings a husky tone to his voice when he remembers the terrible ordeal they endured together.

Somehow, miraculously, some people did survive the Nazis. Steven Nasser survived. He was there. He wrote a book about his experience not to ask for pity or retribution, but to tell the truth that could allow us to save ourselves from ourselves.

For more information please visit **www.mybrothersvoice.com**.

•••

I was born in Budapest, Hungary, in 1931. Everybody called me "Pista." I was born into a good, middle-class family. My parents owned a jewelry store that was established in the Nasser house, a house my grandparents had built in Budapest in 1882. That house still stands, but it's no longer ours because my parents had to sell it during the Great Depression.

At that time we were a down-to-earth, middle-class family. My parents both worked and my older brother, Andris, and I went to school. We'd originally been enrolled in a Jewish school, but when Germany became a threat we switched to another school to try to escape as much atrocity as possible.

It didn't help. The Nazis came and took all my family away—21 people altogether, including my mother and brother. My father had died a few years before, and in a way I have to thank God for that; at least he didn't have to suffer the atrocities.

My aunt's husband, Charles, was drawn into the Hungarian Army in 1943. He went to the Russian front, and when he returned to the Nasser home he found nobody there. I came back several months later, after having been liberated by the Americans and restored from a 72 pound shell to a healthy 138-pound man. When I returned to Budapest my uncle asked what had happened to his family.

I decided to lie. I told him that I didn't know, that we had been separated. But that was not true. My aunt and baby cousin Peter had been massacred in front of me and my mother.

Because of this, until my uncle's death in 1996, I refused to publish an account of what happened. Only after Charles passed away did I have the book published. My brother and I were sent first to Auschwitz, one of the most infamous of the Nazi death camps, but we didn't stay there. In Auschwitz, most people were tattooed, but Andris and I were never tattooed because we were among the 800 people shipped to a different location, Muhldorf, a camp for hard labor. They had no crematorium there, no gas chambers, no tattooing. Instead, they worked and starved you to death.

Not many of the 800 forced laborers from Hungary survived. Fifteen hundred prisoners died of starvation, beatings, or because they just couldn't take it anymore. They were replaced by new prisoners sent from Dachau or Auschwitz. Apparently the capacity of 800 had to be maintained no matter what it took.

Near the end of our time in the camp, very close to liberation, my brother said to me, "Pista, you are going to survive, you have a weapon, and your weapon is your diary. I am confident that you will finish that diary. Take it out and share it with the world." Andris was seventeen at the time; I was fourteen. "Look around at all these people who love their families," he told me. "Look at the younger ones like us—we're all orphans. You can make the difference, Pista. Go out and share with people on the outside and keep on speaking to them. Shake them up about how important it is to have family and freedom."

Then he said, "Pista, I'm going to leave you soon."

"Wait a minute," I said. "You mean you're just going to get up and walk out through the gate, and Mr. Nazi is going to let you out and never come back again?"

"No," he said, "you misunderstand. I feel it in my bones that I am going to die."

That made me very upset, I started to shake him to come to his senses. He jokingly said, "Stop rattling my bones!" I wasn't in the best condition either.

"You have to take it for granted I'm going to leave you here," he said, "and you'll have to make it on your own. We'll all be watching you from above, but if you want to make sure that we're happy looking down at you, you need to have a smile on your face. You have to keep it up and give us the courage to keep smiling back at you until we meet up again and become one big happy family."

Andris died not long before the liberation. That is how the actual story ended, except that as Allied troops got closer the Nazis ran for their lives and gave the camp over to the Wermacht soldiers. Some of them were more human, not like the Nazis. They'd been ordered by the Nazis to put the remaining prisoners in boxcars heading up to the Bavarian Alps, and have them all executed. Thank God they only put us in the boxcars. They didn't want to murder us, or have any more blood on their hands; they hoped that the Americans would find us, and that is what happened.

I was unconscious in the boxcar amongst the bodies of 64 dead people when one of General Patton's soldiers pulled us out and noticed I still had life in me.

When I woke up in the hospital, one of my first questions was, "Where is my diary?"

They didn't know what I was talking about. Unfortunately, the diary I had carefully written under the noses of the Nazis had been beneath my body in the boxcar, and no one noticed. So it got left behind under all those corpses, all the sewage and filth.

One of the doctors came over to me and said, "Hey, son, you were talking to someone. Were you hallucinating?"

"I was talking to my brother, Andris."

"Where is he?"

"He is in heaven."

"But you talk to him?"

"Yes. As a matter of fact I begged to go with him because it looks so peaceful where he is, but he told me, 'Not yet, Pista.'"

Decades later I would use those words—*Not Yet, Pista*—as the title of the stage play and movie script I completed in 2013, with a good friend of mine, educator Ann Raskin. It is now ready for production. Many professional people who read the script realized that my brother's legacy to me should go on to future generations, to make sure people treat each other like human beings. We must never forget what happened in the past. That is history, we can never change it . . . but we are responsible for the future.

That's what I've been doing ever since. So far I've lectured internationally 880 times, but I don't consider what I'm doing anything special. I don't consider myself special.

I'm just keeping my promise to my brother.

The Legacy of
COURAGE

*"Courage is what it takes to stand up and speak; courage is
also what it takes to sit down and listen."*
— WINSTON CHURCHILL

Courage is one of the most powerful words in our
vocabulary and yet is often misunderstood.

There is the courage of the moment, when a
single deed defines a person for posterity. This
is the birthplace of battle-born reputations,
when men and women risk their lives for the
sake of others.

There is also the courage that is born of long
and sustained physical and emotional trauma or
challenges. Pain is the common denominator of
this type of courage, be it sustained through injury,
disease or being subjected to experiences that no
one should be forced to face. Those who have
risen above that suffering and gone on to serve as
the inspiration for others to carry on and achieve
happiness epitomize that brand of courage.

And then there is the courage of thoughts and
ideas that may challenge the conventional wisdom

of the day, and yet when truly examined and understood can better the lives of others.

Each of these examples may be unique, but all share one thread: the Legacy of Courage.

"I answered as any good American citizen would: 'It would be an honor, Mr. President, to serve you and my country in this capacity.'"

KEVIN SAUNDERS

Who is Kevin Saunders? While conducting a United States Department of Agriculture examination of a grain storage facility in Corpus Christi, Kevin was caught in the worst grain elevator explosion in Texas history, and rendered paraplegic. Within a couple of years Kevin turned setback into success, being named "the world's greatest all-around wheelchair athlete" after winning the pentathlon at the World Track & Field Championships.

In 1989 Kevin worked alongside Tom Cruise as a principal actor in *Born on the Fourth of July*, an Academy Award-winning movie directed by Oliver Stone. Kevin has also been featured in over 50 TV commercials promoting fitness, education, health and wellness.

Kevin was the first Paralympian and person with a disability appointed to the President's Council on Physical Fitness, Sports and Nutrition, the only member reappointed to the council by President Clinton, and has been tapped as a constituent expert by President Bush & the PCPFS & Department of Health & Human

Services for a special imitative to improve fitness for children and youth with disabilities.

Kevin pushed his wheelchair over 2,500 miles across America to speak to students, teachers and administrators about the importance of education regarding proper nutrition and fitness. He and his team held "Health & Fitness Summits" with mayors, state governors, other elected officials; and later he wheeled himself through portions of five European nations as an international ambassador for health and fitness. He is the author of *There's Always a Way, Mission Possible, Conversations on Health & Fitness, Blueprint for Success*, and *CENTAUR*, the first wheelchair action-hero comic book. He is currently working on his latest book, *Revolutions: Beating the Fitness Crisis in America, One Push at a Time.*

Kevin has received more than 100 commendations, proclamations and awards, and won hundreds of gold medals competing around the world. He is also a school speaker who established the Wheelchair Success Foundation (WSF), dedicated to providing scholarships to enable people permanently confined to wheelchairs to improve their education, and founded the Fitness 4 All 50 State Tour.

For more information please visit **www.kevinsaunders.com**.

•••

I grew up on a farm in Kansas, thirteen miles from the geographical center of the United States, on land that was homesteaded by my German ancestors in 1880. I grew up working on that farm, so it's probably natural that when I went to college at I majored in agriculture. I played football at Pratt County Community College, but when I transferred to Kansas State the Wildcats weren't very good, so I switched to rugby. I was still playing rugby for the Corpus Christi Rugby Club for fun after I graduated, got married, and became a federal inspector with the United States Department of Agriculture.

As an inspector, my job was to grade the grain being loaded from railroad cars and trucks into grain elevators and to check the elevators to make sure they conformed to safety regulations. In the industry, a "grain elevator" is actually a complex set of structures designed to store and transfer grain for shipment all over the world. An elevator usually includes storage silos, offices, conveyors and other equipment.

Oddly enough, the main safety concern is explosions. You might ask, how can a grain elevator explode? After all, if you toss a match into a bucket of corn or wheat, nothing happens. But things change when grain is being handled and stored in large quantities; it gives off organic dust that's extremely volatile. Mix the right ratio of grain dust and air, close it up in a confined space and add a flame, and you end up with an explosion expanding at 1,500 feet per second—almost as powerful as a nuclear blast. That's why modern elevators are equipped with monitors and dust collection systems, to keep the concentration of dust to a safe level. It's also why they need inspectors.

I'd been on the job for two years in 1981, when I was working at the largest, most modern grain elevator complex in the world. Located on the Gulf Coast in Corpus Christi, Texas, it was a state-of-the-art facility refurbished just a couple of years earlier at a cost of many millions of dollars. The elevator included several dozen silos, each a rebar-reinforced concrete cylinder ten stories tall. Even when divided into three rows packed tightly together, they stretched for a quarter of a mile.

On one end of the complex was an even taller building containing the offices and control room. The control room was like something from NASA, full of monitors and gauges. But there were problems. I'd noted that the dust collection systems weren't working properly, and had pointed that out to the engineer. He hadn't been overly concerned. It would cost too much to fix right then, he told me.

One afternoon at 3:10, I was standing in the government building, holding a clipboard and talking with my supervisor at his desk when I heard a rumble like thunder. But it got louder and louder, deafening. Through a window I saw explosions starting at the far end of the silos and racing toward us up the line, faster and faster. The silos were mostly empty at the time, which meant the dust inside them had plenty of room to mix with air.

Every explosion knocked grain dust loose in the next silo and then set it off, one after the other, making each consecutive explosion bigger than the one before. Later I saw a picture of one of the silos blowing up; it looked like the flame of a blowtorch shooting up and out of the silo at a 45 degree angle and reaching much higher than the silo itself.

The blasts reached us in seconds, but it seemed like slow motion. I saw silos blowing apart like paper, pieces of concrete weighing over a ton flying hundreds of feet through the air. The office floor jumped up and down over a foot, and everything fell off the shelves and wall like we were in a horrendous earthquake. I looked at my supervisor and saw the blood drain out of his face just before he dropped to the floor.

At the same time I was blown up through the roof.

I ended up on the other side of a two-story building next door, over three hundred feet away from the government building. I came down on my head and shoulders on a concrete parking lot. Rescuers found me lying on the concrete with my upper body broken over at the chest the way most people bend at the waist. Blood and spinal fluid were oozing out of my nose, ears and mouth.

Paramedics and doctors started a triage, organizing the victims according to who needed help the most. I wasn't high on the list. In fact they were going to just leave me because my vital signs were so low, but thanks to the Good Lord, one paramedic didn't agree. There weren't enough ambulances and stretchers for all the injured people, even though help was arriving from all along the Gulf Coast. Finally the paramedics just put me on a blown-off door and carried me to a station wagon, and that's how I made it to the intensive care unit at the hospital.

Forty-seven other people were injured in the explosion, and ten people—including my supervisor—died. It was the worst explosion of its kind in both Texas and US history.

I spent almost a year in the hospital, the first month in the ICU while they tried to stabilize me. I had massive head trauma, which doctors thought was enough to kill me, plus internal and external injuries and blunt force trauma to my head and shoulders. Both my scapulas were broken and my lungs had collapsed. It seems that I landed on my head and shoulders, and then my legs flipped over my chest, breaking my body right at the sternum. I overheard the doctors telling my family I had less than a fifty-fifty chance to live.

They drilled holes in my skull to relieve the pressure from the skull fracture I had received upon impact to the concrete, which had caused massive swelling of my brain. Then they had to fight pulmonary embolisms, a fancy word for blood clots in the lung that will kill you if they get to your heart. After that the doctors told me they had good news and bad news. The good news was that I'd survived. The bad news was that my spinal cord had been severed at the level of my chest and I'd be confined for the rest of my life to a wheelchair and have no core balance.

But then things got worse. My wife informed me that she had married a six-foot, 200-pound athlete, not a cripple. Also, she'd expected to never have to work again, but now . . . well, in her opinion I'd ruined her life. Our relationship deteriorated until she was openly physically and verbally abusive.

I hoped that money might make a difference. A top attorney agreed to take my case against the Corpus Christi Public Grain Elevator and almost every company that had supplied them with parts. In the end I was awarded millions of dollars. Although money couldn't bring back the use of my legs, restore the full function of my bladder or bowels, or return to me the athletic life I'd loved, I hoped it might save my marriage. I was wrong. Money can do a lot of things, but it couldn't bring back my wife's love. Whatever feelings she'd had for me withered along with my body. An incredibly messy divorce took years to resolve and left me both disillusioned and broke.

Being told that you'll be in a wheelchair for the rest of your life is bad enough news to throw anyone—single or married, athlete or bookworm—into depression. It's a tough thing to face, and if you don't have the right attitude you won't deal with it well. Bankrupt and bottomed out, I felt that the world had finally defeated me.

But I'd grown up in a Christian home and tried to carry on with those values. I needed that sort of strength in my life if I was going to come back.

Fortunately I had help. One of my oldest friends, Al Buttell, came to see me. We'd been roommates in college until he'd dropped out to join the marine corps. He always was a strong guy; he could do 60 to 80 chin-ups, and he came and encouraged me to not give up. That meant an awful lot to me.

Then there were my rugby friends, Robert Hays and Bruce Acuna. We'd played together on the Corpus Christi Rugby Club before my accident. Sensing that I needed to channel my hurt and frustrations, they did the only thing they knew how to do— they took me to the gym. I wasn't sure I wanted to go, but they wouldn't take no for an answer. They dragged me into the weight room and told me to start lifting and to never give up because "There's Always a Way." When I couldn't do any more reps they'd throw a medicine ball at me as hard as they could, taunting me, daring me to return it with the same force.

From those long afternoons in the gym I learned two things. The first was that exercise and friendship could heal my body and soul in ways that money could not. The second was that it's critical to surround yourself with people who build you up. With good friends on your side, no adversity is too great to overcome.

Once I started working out again, things came together. My brother, Gerald, invited me to come to Georgia where he lived and compete in the Peachtree 10K road race in Atlanta. It's an event that draws more than 50,000 athletes, including both runners and wheelchair athletes, from all around the world.

So I went to Atlanta, where I found a few surprises. First, my wheelchair was an old, bulky, clumsy hospital model, built more like a garbage truck than a speedster. The other competitors' chairs looked like drag-race cars. Second, I didn't even know how long the course was. At that time America was trying to convert from measuring in yards to measuring in meters, so I wasn't sure of the distance. And third, although I'd competed athletically in high school and college, I was so unprepared for what it meant to race in a wheelchair that I didn't even have water with me.

But I lined up anyway, and when the starting gun fired I bore down on my old hospital chair and took off. I poured every ounce of effort into getting a strong start, pumping my arms so hard I thought the tires might leave smoke on the pavement. Driven on by the applause, I didn't notice for a while that something had changed. When I finally looked up I noticed that all the other racers were long gone.

It didn't matter. I was hooked.

In 1984 I found out an exhibition wheelchair race was going to be held in conjunction with the 1984 Olympic Games in Los Angeles, and I set myself the goal of making it to the 1988 games as a competitor. I put up a sign featuring a saying from Arnold Schwarzenegger: "Take the pain that it takes to be a champion." And I went to work. I took the pain, and as a result went on to win gold medals in World Championships, and Paralympics medals in Seoul, Barcelona and Atlanta. At the 1990 World Games in Europe I earned the title of "the world's greatest all around wheelchair athlete" by winning the wheelchair equivalent of the decathlon.

Arnold's quote had been an inspiration to me, but not as much as the man's life. I'd read that when he was a teenager in Austria he once broke into the gym in the wintertime to work out even though it was so cold the bars froze to his hands while he did his reps. Little did I know that soon I'd not only be working with Arnold on the President's Council of Physical Fitness, but become his friend.

My appointment to the council came about because of another man I admired: US Senator Bob Dole, who would later be a presidential candidate. He'd been the commencement speaker at my high school graduation, and I'd never forgotten his story. During World War II he'd been part of a small unit of athletes, including Olympians, trained to ski into enemy locations and attack. On one mission, Bob Dole threw a grenade that hit a tree and bounced back before it exploded. He'd almost died, and his injuries had required more than seven operations to correct. Yet he'd come back from all that pain and damage to achieve great things in his life. What I remembered best was his statement that "can't never accomplished anything. When you say you can't do this or you can't do that, you are absolutely right."

When I began to achieve success and recognition as a wheelchair athlete, my high school named its new track after me. It so happened that the engineer who built the track was a neighbor of Senator Bob Dole's, who saw some information about what had happened to me on TV. In 1989 he flew me out to Washington to meet with President Bush.

In the Oval Office, President Bush told me that he'd seen pictures of me that reminded him of Arnold Schwarzenegger because my arms were so built up—they're basically my legs, after all. He asked if I'd like to be the first person with a disability to join his Council on Physical Fitness and Sports. I answered as any good American citizen would: "It would be an honor, Mr. President, to serve you and my country in this capacity."

At the time I didn't know it, but only twenty people would be selected for the council from a waiting list of over 2,000. Although technically we were part of the Department of Health and Human Services, our meetings were usually held in the White House with the President of the United States and the council's chairman . . . Arnold Schwarzenegger.

When President Bush asked me to join the council, I didn't even realize that one of my all-time idols was in charge of it. I had met Arnold before, at the Republican Convention. At the time he was at his prime and had a bunch of bodyguards, but a friend of mine managed to get close to him and say, "Hey, do you want to meet a man, Kevin Sanders, the wheelchair athlete?"

"Where is he?" Arnold asked.

"He's right behind you," my friend said. I was trying to weave my way through the crowd. "He's right behind you!" my friend kept yelling, but Arnold didn't see me until I almost ran into his shins with my wheelchair.

I had a gift for Arnold. A girl I knew from the gym was originally from Austria. I'd told her I was going to meet Arnold, and asked her if she could find an Austrian hat. Her mom still lived in Austria, so she got the hat and put a bunch of Austrian pins on one side. When I pulled it out from under my wheelchair and held it out to Arnold I said, "Do you know what this is?"

He smiled. "Yah! . . . It's an Austrian hiking hat!"

I got to thank him personally for inspiring me; helping me get those extra reps in the gym, keeping me pushing harder and further. I told him how, because I was paralyzed from the chest down, I had to figure out new ways to do certain exercises, using Velcro and all kinds of stuff to rig things up so I could do an exercise sitting down or strapped to a piece of equipment, and that he was my inspiration for that creativity.

Years later, I took some friends to meet him. His office was nice and neat; he's a detail-oriented person and a hard worker, like

Senator Bob Dole. "There are no shortcuts to success," as Senator Dole had told my high school graduating class, and Arnold lives his life by that, too.

Right off his office he had an Austrian room like you'd see in a regular Austrian home. When I looked into it I thought about the hat I'd given Arnold so many years ago . . . and there it was, sitting on a bench. What struck me was that the hat was in better condition than it had been in when I first gave it to him twenty years earlier.

A lot of things changed for me during those years. I did a "Live Your Dreams" tour at schools and gave away some of the gold medals I'd won to kids in the children's hospitals who had lost their legs or suffered other kinds of injuries. I would encourage them to never give up or let their disabilities stop them. What state of mind did they want to have? Did they want to be a contributor to the world or be dependent on the world?

I've had over 5,000 speaking engagements and visited over 2,000 schools. I've had kids come up to me and say they'd been about to drop out of school when they heard me speak. Not only did they stay in school, most of them went on to graduate from college, and some opened their own businesses and became very successful in life. Those are the kinds of stories that really touch me—they make me think there must be something coming through me from above to touch somebody's life like that. It's a humbling honor to have such an impact on young people that you help them to totally change the course of their lives and turn it into something positive.

I have to give the same credit to the people I got to know. Not only people like Senator Bob Dole and Arnold Schwarzenegger, but regular guys like my friend Al. People who support you and show an interest and contribute to your recovery and help you go on to greater heights.

I didn't die that day in Corpus Christi. It wasn't my time. But not everyone gets a second chance in life, so be sure to make the best of your first one!

AUTHOR'S NOTE: The idea that Legacy Moments can extend powerfully over long spans of time is perfectly illustrated by the way Kevin Saunders drew strength, at his moment of greatest need, from a story he'd heard years before about a man he had never met: Senator Bob Dole.

But as the following story shows, Kevin and the senator would come to serve as inspirations for one another—a true testament to the enduring power of Legacy.

"I'd say you could go through your entire life
supporting others with disabilities."

BOB DOLE

W**ho is Bob Dole?** Robert Joseph "Bob" Dole is an attorney and retired United States senator from Kansas. He served in the Senate from 1969–1996, part of that time as United States Senate majority leader, where he set a record as the longest-serving Republican leader.

He was the Republican nominee in the 1996 US presidential election and the Republican vice presidential nominee in the 1976 US presidential election.

Mr. Dole has received national acclaim for his leadership on behalf of the disadvantaged and disabled, and in 2007 was appointed by President George W. Bush as a co-chair of the commission to investigate problems at Walter Reed Army Medical Center.

For more information please visit **www.alston.com**.

•••

I grew up in the small town of Russell, Kansas, where I played football and basketball in high school. Later I attended college at the University of Kansas. After Pearl Harbor was attacked I enlisted in the reserves, and in less than a year I was called to active duty. I served in the 75th Infantry Division for about three months before I was selected to go to Officer Candidate School. I was shipped to Italy as a 2nd lieutenant and spent Christmas of 1944 in the 24th Replacement Depot with a number of other soldiers.

The next year, I was transferred to a post in northern Italy where there was a German machine gun nest. I was ordered to lead an assault against it, and during the attack I was severely wounded: shattered right shoulder, fractured vertebrae, paralysis from the neck down, shrapnel throughout my body, and a damaged kidney. Although I spent three years in the hospital, I lost the kidney and the use of my right arm. I still don't have good feeling in my left hand, and that arm is rather weak.

When I got out of the hospital, I used my G.I. Bill to go to college. I chose Arizona State University because of the climate, but I wanted to go to law school, so after a year I returned to Kansas and attended law school at Washburn University in Topeka.

I practiced law with a friend until 1959, when I ran for Congress and was elected to the House. Eight years later, I was elected to the Senate, which I left voluntarily in 1996 to campaign for the presidency.

Throughout my life, I have been inspired by the actions of many people. My parents, to begin with, and all the doctors, nurses, therapists and occupational therapists who helped me through my long recovery.... I remember in particular one Lucy

Kamman, an occupational therapist who got me to do a lot of things and helped me with my left hand.

But my real hero is another Kansan, Dwight D. Eisenhower. I have always considered him my inspiration; he affected me with his leadership qualities and ability to get things done.

I met him a couple of times—first when I was in the hospital, later at the White House and then again in Canada, but unfortunately our interaction was limited. Even so, I learned from him the values of leadership, honesty, integrity, and never giving up…. He was a man who persevered through the darkest days—something I've always admired about him.

I'm pleased to be involved in the current planning of the Eisenhower Memorial here in Washington, D.C.

Another personal inspiration of mine is John Kemp, who was born without arms and legs but gets around well with prosthetic limbs. I met him in Washington years ago, and afterwards I think I became involved in just about every disability issue that came before Congress. Another inspiring individual I've encountered is Kevin Saunders, an athlete who was disabled in a terrible explosion in a grain elevator. His perseverance is admirable. Making the most of one's unique abilities is paramount to me.

Because of my interest in the disability community, I'm currently helping to garner support for the convention on the Rights of Persons with Disabilities, a treaty that would protect disabled Americans who travel abroad. I'm crossing my fingers for a few additional votes in the Senate.

"There's no better therapy than helping
someone else with a disability."

URBAN MIYARES

Who is Urban Miyares? Urban Miyares is a nationally recognized entrepreneur, blinded and multi-disabled Vietnam veteran, motivational/inspirational speaker and lecturer, author, inventor and patent holder, media personality, world-class disabled athlete and sailor. He is the president of the Disabled Businesspersons Association, a San Diego-based, volunteer-driven 501(c)(3) public charity he founded in 1985.

In 2011, Miyares became a content expert for the Hadley School for the Blind's Forsythe Center for Entrepreneurship as well as the school's new Veterans Outreach specialist.

Urban Miyares and the Disabled Businesspersons Association are now recognized as one of the nation's leading authorities on the self-employment of people with disabilities, having assisted thousands in their entrepreneurial endeavors. Among his many professional activities, Urban is co-founder and director of Challenged America, a leader in the field of adaptive sailing as a therapeutic, rehabilitation activity; director of the National

Disabled Veterans Business Center and Special Kids In Business—the latter an innovative San Diego after-school entrepreneur and mentor program for school-aged children with disabilities. He is also founder and principal in a number of business ventures and other community programs.

Urban is the host of Biz @ 9, a monthly webinar on non-traditional self-employment.

Urban and JoAnn, his wife of 43 years, live in San Diego. They have one son who, with his wife, have given them four grandchildren.

For more information please visit **www.challengedamerica. com**.

•••

I was born in 1947 in a little brownstone apartment in New York City. It was a tenement, what they called a railroad flat; from where I slept in the back I could see the front window through the kitchen and living room. My parents slept on a fold-out couch.

Yet all around us were wealthy people. Back then the city was broken up: go two blocks and you're in a German neighborhood; go two blocks the other way and you're in a Slavic or Italian neighborhood.

My dad was in the restaurant business, food service, bartending; and at night he dealt cards at illegal poker games up on Amsterdam Avenue. There was a pizzeria there, and they held poker games in a back room. I grew up in that environment.

My grandmother lived next door. She was a well-known Jewish chef, although we are not Jewish—my father is Spanish-Cuban, and my mother a combination of German, Russian, and Greek. When I went to visit my grandmother, my name, Urban Miyares, became "Irving Meyers." That actually worked for me in high school because back then the wealthy kids in the neighborhood went to the same school I did, and it seemed like a lot of the girls I liked were Jewish and wealthy. So "Irving Meyers" worked great.

During the summer my friends and I were juvenile delinquents—what they call "at-risk youth" nowadays—and I'd go from Jones Memorial to Lennox Hill neighborhood centers in Manhattan. People would come and take us in.

When I was seven years old I was invited to a yacht club, where I fell in love with sailing. I'd go out on the water whenever I got the chance: South Bay, Great South Bay, Long Island Sound. There weren't many opportunities for a kid like me back then, but the love never went away, and later it would become a crucial part of my life.

Everything changed in 1967, when I was nineteen. First, I got married to JoAnn, a girl I'd known for six years. We had a short honeymoon because I immediately got drafted and sent to a special army school, the Non-Commissioned Officers Academy. It had just been developed because too many infantry platoon leaders, sergeants and officers were getting wounded or killed in Vietnam, which forced the army to promote people who weren't ready for what they were going to face. So they created a special academy where we went through demolition and basic range training, so by the time we got to Vietnam we were prepared to be squad leaders or platoon sergeants. The down side was that once I got to Vietnam, instead of being kept in the rear for two weeks until I acclimated, on my second day in-country I was sent out on a night ambush.

We saw some action. Nothing hot and heavy that first night; five or ten seconds of someone taking shots at us and then disappearing. But it was intense.

Then I started getting sick. Vomiting, blurred vision, couldn't eat. At sick call they looked for malaria but didn't find it. They thought the heat was getting to me. All I could keep down was fluids. I fell in love with orange soda, and of course beer. Warm or cold—it didn't matter to me. "Drink more fluids," they said. "No problem," I said.

But there was a price. I'd go out on an operation and have to stop and pee in a rice paddy. There I was, leading men in combat while I felt like I had the world's worst case of the flu. It got so bad I had problems understanding things. I couldn't sleep at night.

In sick call I got a second diagnosis: battle fatigue. I was seeing too much action too soon, they said, and gave me 24 hours at base camp to recuperate. I did that, but a few days later I ended up in sick call again. This time they diagnosed a peptic ulcer, and gave me Maalox. The bottle fit perfectly into the M-16 pouch. It was built for that thing. Other guys in the platoon would carry Maalox for me because I was drinking it like water, or maybe warm beer.

But when we came back from the next operation I was sicker than ever. I was losing weight, my belt buckle going in and in and my pants falling down. The sergeant major told me, "The company commander says if you don't stop going to sick call, they're going to bust you." They thought I was malingering, trying to get out of duty.

The next time we had an operation I had a tough time even waking up for the briefing. I was dizzy, everything was spinning.

My platoon was going to be the lead platoon, the point platoon. I don't remember much about it. I remember helicopters and walking along a rice paddy. I remember falling, and someone taking my backpack and someone else taking the M-60 ammunition I had strapped across my chest. "Don't worry, Sarge," they said. "We'll take care of you."

Then there were mortar shells coming in and machine guns going off, and I fell face first into the rice paddy. That was the last time I saw those men.

I woke up in the Saigon Military Hospital, surrounded by tubes. The first thing I did was lift the sheet to see if I still had my legs. They were there, but apart from that I didn't know what was going on. I just knew there were tubes all over me and that I felt a little better, but far from well.

After a couple of episodes of waking up and falling asleep, I was finally told what was wrong with me: I had Type I diabetes. I'd gone into a diabetic coma out there in the rice paddy.

But that wasn't the worst of the story. When a guy from my outfit came to check on me he said, "Guess where they found you before they brought you in here?"

"Where?"

"In a body bag."

"What?"

"Someone thought you were dead and put you in a body bag. You were piled with all the others for two days."

I didn't hear the whole story for another 38 years, after I located the medic who'd found me in that body bag. His name was Bryan Leet, US Army combat medic. He told me that the medical base camp had been located in a rubber plantation. When the body bags were brought in they got thrown into a shed out in the sun until someone could deal with them. After all the wounded were taken care of, Bryan and another medic were assigned to toe-tag the dead soldiers as best they could. Opening a body bag was a terrible thing. I knew that from personal experience, from being out in the field after a firefight. You'd throw an unattached in the bag; I remember one time somebody threw in a head, somebody's head that had been lying out in the field. So when you open the bags they're generally filled with blood.

But when Bryan opened up my bag it was dry inside. No blood. He felt for a pulse and found it, and they threw me in a chopper. Bryan was with me maybe five minutes, but he saved my life.

I stayed in Saigon Hospital for a week and a half, then got shipped to Japan. They couldn't get my diabetes under control. This was in 1968, when diabetes was basically a death sentence. For insulin injections we used glass syringes, which we had to boil, and the needles were thick. We had to sharpen them with emery boards every day. I was taking six, eight, ten, twelve shots a day—they couldn't give me enough insulin. I was insulin resistant.

I wound up in Valley Forge Hospital in Pennsylvania. I remember lying in bed, angry that I wasn't in Vietnam. I wanted to go back so bad. I couldn't even remember the names of the men in my platoon on that last operation; we'd only been together for two days. But I'd been told that none of them had survived. So I had this guilt—"Why am I still alive?"

I was in the hospital so long they put me on leave so I could go home on weekends, or for a week at a time. My wife got pregnant right away. As for me, the doctors said I had twenty years left to live at best.

Back then, if you had any physical condition that resembled a complication of diabetes, they blamed it on the diabetes. For example, I started having trouble with my vision; I couldn't read road signs when I drove even though at an exam my vision tested at 20/20. I had problems with my back and couldn't feel my legs. That started with my feet—I just couldn't feel them. About a week later the numbness was up to my knees, and then my thighs. They gave me a nerve conduction test, where they stick needles in your leg and shoot you with electricity, and I was told I had ninety percent nerve damage from the waist down. Walking was difficult. Painful.

And it was all because of diabetes . . . until 1978 or 1979, when information about the long-term effects of Agent Orange started coming out. Agent Orange is the chemical defoliant they used in Vietnam, and these days doctors name it as a presumed cause of 17 different illnesses, including Parkinson's disease, Type II diabetes—I had Type I—and a number of cancers.

In 1984, after a couple of years of being legally blind, I went totally blind. My eyesight loss was partly due to retinopathy, which is diabetes-related, but I also have optic neuropathy—no blood in my optic nerves. They believe it's the same as the neuropathy in my legs.

It just goes on. I've had a kidney transplant. Then there's PTSD. Back then they diagnosed it as manic-depression and put us on lithium.

Fortunately my son was born healthy, although Agent Orange has been proven to be potentially responsible for a lot of birth defects, including spina bifida.

Shortly after leaving the hospital I got my military discharge. They mailed it to me. Welcome home. I didn't know I was entitled to any benefits. All us vets thought that was the procedure: just sign the forms and get out. That was the way it had been for my father after his service in World War II. He used to tell us stories about it when he was drunk, but I didn't know how true they were. I didn't talk about my Vietnam experience at all, not even to my wife.

I didn't tell my co-workers, either. A friend of mine got me hired on as an apprentice at the Wall Street company he worked for, but at the office I never mentioned Vietnam. The war wasn't very popular. So I'd just bite my tongue and go to work, hobbling because of the pain in my legs.

But one day after I'd been there a couple of months, the subway was running behind schedule and I came in late. The secretary told me, "They want to see you in the manager's office."

A gentleman in a three-piece banker's suit was waiting for me, holding a handful of needles. "We found these in your desk. What's up?"

"I have diabetes," I said. "I'm a Vietnam veteran."

He frowned. "We're not having any needle-touting, baby-killing Vietnam vets working for this company. Harry, take care of it."

So I had to go home and tell my pregnant wife I'd just been fired.

What was I going to do now? I was 21 years old and had been told I had twenty years left to live at most. I had no education; I'd barely gotten through high school. And in addition to my physical ailments I was still suffering from survivor's guilt. I considered suicide but decided I couldn't kill myself and make my unborn child deal with that legacy.

Instead, my wife and I decided we'd just live one day at a time.

With that in mind I started a business with a gentleman I met at a lumberyard, Jerry Sullivan. He was a carpenter, and to me, "Sullivan and Urban" sounded like "US Building and Supply." We did house framing. I didn't even know how to hold a hammer at first, but Jerry showed me. We framed a lot of homes in New Jersey and Lakewood and Bayville and Tom's River.

But things didn't work out. Jerry was a Southern Baptist: no drinking, lots of Bible study, and when it's sunny you have to pound nails, not take the day off—especially in Jersey, where the winters are long and cold. You had to get the houses framed so you could work inside during the winter. So someone in Jerry's church bought up my interest in the business. The money I got barely covered the bills, but I went on to form other businesses, including a little hardware store in upstate New York.

But I was still having problems with PTSD and being around people, and my medical problems kept getting worse. Finally I fell off a roof because my back and legs hurt so much that I said, "One of these days, when I can prove that a veteran is severely, catastrophically disabled, I'm going to help them help themselves."

The hardware store failed because I was in such pain I couldn't get to work. My doctor told me I needed to get to a warm, dry climate.

"My in-laws just moved to Albuquerque, New Mexico," I said.

"Well, it's certainly warmer there," he said. Clearly he didn't know how cold it gets in Albuquerque in the winter, and neither did we—but we moved anyway.

In New Mexico I tried the insurance business and didn't like it much even though I did fairly well at it. So when I found a restaurant that was for sale I took it over and had my family help work it. My mother-in-law happened to be a wonderful cook. Her recipes were Slovak, and between that my grandmother's German and Russian recipes we had enough to get started. We opened as a small restaurant, but two and a half years later we had a place that seated 440 people.

In 1997, thanks to more medical issues coupled with family members not being interested in keeping the restaurant going while I recovered, we sold the place and moved to San Diego. But meanwhile I had met a wonderful gentleman—one of the finest people in my life. As I always say, there people out there who either by their actions, their negativity, or what they do to other people, set an example I don't want to follow. Then there are those who say, "Here, let me help you," and reach out a hand pull you over a hurdle. Those people, call them angels, have been instrumental in my life at particular times.

My friend and I started a number of businesses even though my health kept getting worse. By that time I was totally blind, but I borrowed $1,700 on my credit card and started a manufacturing business to produce an invention of mine. Two years later we were doing government contracting work and making over $10 million annually in sales. I became *Inc. Magazine*'s Entrepreneur of the Year, and had two presidents of the United States invite my wife and me to lunch.

One day as I came back from blind rehab a gentlemen I had been in business with a couple of times previously approached me and said, "Urban, you ready to go to work?"

"What can I do?"

"You can still answer the phone, can't you, dammit?"

"Yeah. . . ."

So I started there, and we wound up launching a couple of very successful businesses. That man now volunteers here at our charity.

Best of all, in 1985 I was finally able to honor my pledge to help other disabled veterans. With money I got from selling one of my businesses I launched a pilot program to help disabled vets get into business themselves. Originally I intended to take one or two vets under my wing and mentor them, but one of them did so well we actually went into partnership together, and he eventually bought out my interest for a dollar. And that was it. If I put $10,000 in, I want you to put $10,000. If I work forty hours a week, I want you to work forty hours a week.

That first year I mentored three vets, two with spinal cord injuries and one with low vision. By the next year I was working with 30-something vets, and after that the thing just started rolling. Word got out in the veteran community that there was this guy who was winning all these business awards, a disabled vet like them, who wanted to work with them and try to help them. I got so many requests that in 1990 I started a non-profit organization to handle them all. For eleven years I paid the expenses of that organization out of my own pocket. Even today, although I get donations, I still personally fund fifty to seventy-five percent of the charity. It's diversified into five distinct programs that service more than 3,000 people a year. One of the programs, Challenged America, is a free, adaptive sailing program for people with disabilities. They come to San Diego from around the world to participate.

We're considered the pioneer in therapeutic sailing, which is exactly what it sounds like. It goes back to the love of sailing I'd found as a kid, when someone helped me out by putting me in a boat. Therapeutic sailing is a way to get someone who's either never sailed before, or someone with experience who's become disabled, to learn to handle a sailboat, to master that skill and get out in nature having fun. Let's face it, people don't like going to clinical therapy or to the gym, working with weights and all that. It gets boring and painful. But sailing is such a safe, passive sport, even though your body's always in motion—especially with small boats. As for people with hidden disabilities like PTSD, well, to sail you have to get your mind off everything else, otherwise the boat's not going anywhere. People learn that. They also discover a sense of security. Out on the water you don't have to worry about someone jumping out of a hole at you, or stepping around a blind corner and shooting at you.

As a result, a lot of PTSD vets, including some who served in Iraq and Afghanistan, come here. Many of them become volunteers. There's no better therapy than helping someone else with a disability.

Challenged America services anywhere from 500 to 1,200 people a year. They come from all over the world because of the technology we offer.

Imagine a gentleman with Duchenne muscular dystrophy. The only thing he can move is his eyes—left and right; he can't move his head. And maybe his thumb—a half-inch, either way. And he's on a ventilator. Imagine this man sailing a 16-foot boat by himself. Well, he can do that here. We invented the fiber-optic technology for that.

Then there's our National Disabled Veterans Business Center. Despite their impairments, most disabled vets are mentally and physically capable of going on in life. They might get depressed once in a while, or maybe they have a leg missing. But put a prosthetic leg on them and they'll probably run faster than they ever did with their real leg. Here, we focus on people who are catastrophically disabled. We do educational programs, lectures, seminars, and workshops on self-employment of the disabled.

We also have a program called Special Kids in Business that we developed with San Diego high schools for kids with developmental and learning disabilities. Generally these kids are on SSI, supplementary income, because they were born disabled or got that way before they were eighteen. And most of them will stay on SSI the rest of their lives.

I wanted to work with these kids to see how we could get them back to work. Not all of them are going to have their own businesses, of course; some of their IQs are down. But they are work-capable. So we created Special Kids in Business to help them. We meet once a week—a mentor-type program. That's my true love. I just love working with these kids. They're so innocent, but a lot of them become criminals. Because of their mental disabilities, other kids or adults use them as pawns to sell drugs. Hopefully we've helped some of them; we have some wonderful success stories of these kids leading fulfilling lives. And we have an eighty-five percent back-to-work success rate.

It's about being a role model.

When I was a kid growing up in New York City, my idol was the famous baseball player Mickey Mantle. I remember watching him hit switch-handed at the plate. I tried to imitate him—the way he swung his bat. But when I was about eleven years old and working with a gentlemen delivering restaurant supplies after school, something happened. We were unloading supplies at the stadium lounge outside Yankee Stadium, and who did I see at the bar? Whitey Ford, Enos Slaughter . . . and my hero, Mickey Mantle. And he was drunk. Drunk as a skunk. The others were trying to get him up because it was three in the afternoon and they had a game that night. He was slobbering like any bum on a New York City street. I mean, talk about shattering a dream.

Fortunately I had other heroes in my life. My parents, whose work ethics influenced me. And my grandmother. She couldn't speak English or write at all—you know, an immigrant from

Eastern Europe who came here right after World War I. But she was my love, more of a mother to me than my own mom was. My mother was very loving but didn't really know how to be a parent. We never said "I love you" at home. But I always knew that my grandmother was there.

But the biggest influence in my life was undoubtedly Vietnam and the guys I knew there who never made it back. They are my personal heroes and always have been. From the time I was lying in the hospital in Pennsylvania recuperating from my two days in a body bag, I wanted to do something for the guys I'd shared ground with, sitting cross-legged during ambushes. They were good men. Black, Puerto Rican, Caucasian; all ethnicities. But so many of them didn't come back home. So I thought, *They're not here to do anything. I gotta do something for them.*

Those men motivate me—and believe me, I get beat up quite a bit for what I do. For example, we recently entered a boat in a yacht race to Hawaii. We'd spent almost a year modifying the boat so it could be handled by a two-man crew with catastrophic disabilities. I spent $75,000 out of my own pocket for this race, but at the last moment we were told we couldn't compete. We'd qualified, like every other crew out of more than 300 sailors who entered. We'd qualified. I qualified personally, like everyone else. But hours before the race, the officials gave me a letter that said, *We will not accept your entry because you're blind.*

Those race officials were scared that something would happen to us because there would be only two of us on the boat. They surrendered to an unfounded fear. An attitude. Never mind that I personally have over 30,000 offshore racing miles under my keel. Never mind that I've sailed on America's Cup boats; I've raced them. Never mind that in 2003 I skippered the first boat crewed by people with severe disabilities—quadriplegics, paraplegics, amputees; half of them vets—across the Pacific Ocean.

A similar thing happened in downhill skiing. I'm a former world champion Alpine skier—the world's fastest totally blind skier, clocked at 63 miles an hour in turns on a downhill. I retired in 1991 because I got frustrated with the Paralympic team. Prior to the 1992 Paralympics held in Albertville, France, I had broken a leg, and the Paralympic team said, "You're not allowed to ski with a cast on your leg." Can you imagine being told you're too disabled to compete in a disabled sport? To make matters worse, I'd already beaten everyone in the world with a cast on my leg just a week before. My guide was Bill Johnson—I called him "Crazy Bill"—the first American ever to win an Olympic gold medal in downhill skiing.

It didn't matter. They decided to disallow totally blind skiers anyway because the downhill slope was too severe.

So I keep getting these negatives, and sometimes I just want to quit. But one of my sayings is that freedom isn't always free, and some of us are still paying for it. I mean that. Forget Vietnam and freedom and serving your country. I figure I'm running point for the guys who never had the chance to do it for themselves. So when people think I'm crazy, I tell them, "That's right; I'm service-connected crazy. I've got PTSD."

That's actually one of my speeches: how to use PTSD positively. One of the symptoms of the syndrome is that you can't sleep at night. Okay, so go work on your emails, dammit. Or write articles. Another symptom is depression. You know, I get depressed on Thursday at two o'clock. That's when I set up my depression time. So if I feel depressed on Monday, I wait until Thursday at two p.m. before I address it. It's a meeting, but the feeling always disappears by then.

I do lectures on these things. I keep busy. I reach out. More than ten thousand people a year hear me speak. I don't sleep well. My wife tells me that once every four days or so I'll crash for six or seven hours. Then I'll go two days without sleeping. I just work constantly. Is the charity work I'm doing self-serving? You bet. It's given me a psychological boost; I look forward to every day; I look forward to telling my story about this. I'm healthier today than I was when I came back in 1968 from Vietnam. Yes, I've had my thyroid removed; I've had a stroke; I still have balance problems. But it's been forty-five years since the doctors told me I had twenty years to live. I'm in better shape than my diabetes doctor, and he has Type I diabetes.

My family has probably suffered because of it, at least financially. We could have retired years ago—but I've seen those who've retired. They're dead now, or in bad shape. I still don't have a gray hair on my head, as far as I can see. I checked this morning. I looked in the mirror.

So in this respect my Vietnam experience was the best thing that ever happened to me. Of course I'd prefer for the guys I served with to still be alive. I wish I could see their families, their kids and spouses and loved ones, and help them out. I know what it means to take a life, so I'd like to do the same thing with the families of the enemy dead. I'd love to help them, too, and say I'm sorry.

But that's it. I just keep on moving. I keep finding new answers to those questions I ask everyone else: "What's your encore? What're you going to do next?"

"Dad, when I'm running, it feels like
my disability disappears."

DICK HOYT

Who is Dick Hoyt? Team Hoyt is the father-and-son athletic team of Dick and Rick Hoyt. After being diagnosed shortly after birth as a spastic quadriplegic with cerebral palsy, Rick was expected by doctors to have no chance of being rehabilitated or leading a fulfilling life. Instead, he and his father Dick began competing together in long-distance runs and triathlons all over the world, helping those who are physically disabled to become active members of the community and inspiring everyone to realize that "Yes, you can!"

In the spring of 1977, Rick Hoyt told his father, Dick Hoyt, that he wanted to participate in a 5-mile benefit run for a lacrosse player who had been paralyzed in an accident. Although he was far from being a long-distance runner, Dick agreed to push Rick in his wheelchair. They finished all five miles, coming in next to last. That night Rick told his father, "Dad, when I'm running, it feels like I'm not handicapped."

This was just the beginning of what would become over 1,000 races completed, including marathons, duathlons and triathlons.

In 1989 Rick and Dick formed the Hoyt Foundation, which aspires to build the individual character, self-confidence and self-esteem of America's disabled young people through inclusion in all facets of daily life, including in family and community activities, sports, at home, in schools, and in the workplace.

For more information please visit **www.teamhoyt.com**.

•••

My name is Dick Hoyt, and I'm one of ten children. (My father wanted a baker's dozen but my mother told him that her machine broke down.) We all had blond hair and blue eyes, and were known as the healthiest family that attended our local school.

We didn't grow up in a big house. Privacy was limited to curtains separating our beds. The entire family used one bathroom, yet we never fought. That alone was amazing! Still, our neighborhood description remained "the cleanest, healthiest family" around.

I was a fairly good athlete and made the varsity team as a freshman. With only 50 kids in that class, our team took whatever talent they could find. There were eleven players on the football team, so we had to play both ways and no one could afford to get injured. At the time, the only sports taught at my high school were baseball, football, and basketball. As captain of the baseball team and captain of the football team, it was my responsibility to set an example. I played first string on the basketball team, and, during my senior year, I actually tried out for the Yankees as a catcher. As a student, I was classic. I was the type that showed up to school early, who wanted to raise the flag in the morning and take it down before I went home. My schedule worked for this task as well, since I stayed at school until after I finished football practice or participated in whatever was going on. I was also a straight A student, at least up until the 6th grade when a growing interest in sports and girlfriends took its toll on my study time.

As for college, I didn't prepare myself at all. Instead of putting my nose to the grindstone, I maximized other options. I had my girlfriends do my homework for me! They got mad because I got better grades than I deserved, but after my high school graduation, my "fiddling grasshopper" mentality finally caught up with me. I got really scared, wanting to know what I was going to do, how I would take care of myself. My brother-in-law, Paul Sweeney, who married my sister Alice, suggested I go into the military. In a roundabout way, I did. Instead of going in as an active duty soldier, the powers that be suggested I join the National Guard.

So I trained with the Army National Guard and attended basic training. And I loved it! I really ate it up. During these years they gave you all kinds of tests, checking to see what career field you were most suited for. My highest scores were in electronics, so I went over to Texas and ended up working for Nike Ajax and Nike Hercules, the missile air defense company for the East Coast. One of my commanders thought I would do well in the military and suggested that I go through the OCS. I did so and was commissioned. Then they closed up the Nike Ajax and Nike Hercules missiles, so my job was eliminated. Still, I was full-time and wore my uniform every day, just like an active duty soldier.

Next I was transferred out to OCS Air Force Base in McCabe. This caused me to transfer over to the Air National Guard from the Army National Guard. At first I was excited about this, because the rumor was that McCabe would be used as a storage point for our nuclear weapons. But they had a big scare and these plans were dumped. The result? My job was eliminated again! But, long story short, I went to Westfield, Massachusetts, and ended up putting 35 years into the military.

But that only covers my professional experience. Backtracking a bit, I made one of my most important choices fresh out of high school. When I graduated I married Judy, my best friend. She was the head cheerleader and I was the captain of the football team. I was 19 and she was 18. It was the beginning of our family. Our boy, Rick, came into the world when I was 20 and Judy was 19. There were problems with Rick, so I had to hold a couple of jobs to pay medical bills. This actually worked out well. We prospered because I held down the two jobs, and we built our own house. With one of my jobs I became a mason. I had my own masonry company, where I used to build foundations and pull floaties through the chimneys and sidewalks. I took Rick with me when I was building these chimneys. I would climb up the ladder with the bricks and the mortar, and I had a little chair that let me take him up with me. He cheerfully watched me build the chimneys, because I usually worked alone, and this was part of his time with Dad.

Rick was different, special and challenged. He had been a very active baby, even when he was in the process of being born. During the birth he turned himself over and the umbilical cord got caught around his neck. In this position it took several minutes before the doctors untangled him from it and oxygen again reached his brain. The lack of oxygen at this formative age caused brain damage known as "cerebral palsy."

At the time we knew there was something wrong with Rick, but we didn't know exactly what. The doctor made an appointment for us to see a specialist when Rick was eight months old. The specialist took all kinds of tests and kept saying that Rick was so brain damaged there was no way for him to function. "Forget Rick," he said. "Put him away. Put him in an institution. He's going to be nothing but a vegetable for the rest of his life." The family joke is that Rick is now 51 years old and we're still trying to figure out what kind of vegetable he is....

But on that terrible day we drove home crying. We talked about not putting Rick away, promised that we were going to bring him home and bring him up like any other child. This is exactly what we have done. Rick has been mainstreamed and included all of his life. Rick not only graduated from public high school, he graduated from Boston University and lives all by himself in his own apartment. And he and I have competed in over 1,100 athletic events over the past 34 years.

He has been a shining example and a joy!

Many of my accomplishments come directly from the opportunity to love and care for Rick. When I turned 40 years old, Rick was attending a school in Westfield, Massachusetts. His gym teacher got him involved in all the gym activities with the other children. This coach was also the basketball coach at Westfield State College, and used to take Rick to the basketball games. At one of the games they announced that one of the ball players had had an accident and been paralyzed from the waist down. They were organizing a charity road race to raise money to pay his medical bills.

Well, Rick came home from that game and told me all about it. He said, "Dad, I have to do something for him. I want to let him know that life goes on even though he is paralyzed; I want to run in this race!"

I was 40 years old and not a runner, although I used to run at least three times a week just to keep my weight down. All we had was a heavy wheelchair that was prescribed to fit to Rick's body. It was hard to just push him in it; it would be a real challenge running with it. But we went down to the race and they gave us the number double zero. It was a five mile race. But when the gun went off Rick and I took off running with all of the other runners. I would have been glad to have gone back to the car, but we finished the whole race, crossing the finish line next to last. Afterward the gym teacher's wife took a picture of us, and Rick had the biggest smile you ever saw in your life! When we got home he wrote in his computer, "Dad, when I'm running, it feels like my disability disappears."

Team Hoyt was born!

Rick's computer entry was a very powerful message to me. For somebody confined to a wheelchair, who can't talk and has limited use of his arms and legs, to say that when he runs his disability disappears? It was amazing. From that point on he called himself Free Bird, because now he was free and able to be out there competing and running with everyone else. He actually had a sign made up that said Free Bird that he attached to his running chair. By the way, "Free Bird" is also one of his favorite songs.

But after that first race, I had to face one problem. *I* was disabled! I didn't know how many muscles in your body could ache; I could barely walk for two weeks. So I told Rick that if we were going to continue running, we were going to have to get a chair built that was lighter so I would not be hurting as badly. In pursuit of this chair we travelled to Gretchen Mile, New Hampshire, and met an engineer. We told him what we wanted for a chair and he got some old pipes and some old tubes and welded them together. Then we got an insert for Rick to sit in. This chair had one wheel in the front and two in the back—it was the forerunner of today's baby joggers.

If only I'd thought to patent that chair . . .

A bike company was supposed to work with us, and I told them that they had to build this chair because others were going to want to buy one. They walked away. Five years later there were baby joggers everywhere and people bought them. Rick and I were still thinking about getting a running chair built so we could compete together. We took our first running chair over to our first official race, in Springfield, Massachusetts. When we arrived nobody came over to us, no one talked to us, and nobody wanted us in the race. But the overall race director said we could run. It was a 10K race, 6.2 miles, with over 300 runners. Rick and I finished in 150th place out of the 300 runners.

After that we ran many races in many different towns. People started coming up to us and talking to us. They noticed that Rick had a personality and sense of humor. He liked to be in the middle of things. He always had a big smile on his face and his arms up in the air. We thought it was great.

Others were less impressed. I started getting letters and phone calls from families with disabled people. Surprisingly, they were very upset with me. They claimed I was dragging my disabled son around while seeking glory for myself. What they didn't realize was that *he* was the one dragging *me* through all these races.

That fall, Rick and I sat down and talked about what we wanted to do the following year. We decided that we wanted to run the Boston Marathon, so we applied to the Boston Athletic Association. They turned us down. They said that because we were different we couldn't run in the main event, but they had a wheelchair division. We applied through them, but they also turned us down. They also said, "No. You are different from us. The people in this division push their wheelchairs themselves." Now we were different because I was pushing Rick! However, they allowed us to line up behind them and run. So that was what we did in 1981.

I put a plastic water container behind Rick's head, with a straw attached to it. I didn't want to cause any waves by going in and out of the water stops and attracting attention. But it was like trying to drink while bending over. It really didn't work. If you've seen chickens drink, they peck then throw their heads back to swallow. It was terribly awkward for me. Today we've been in so many races that we can get in and out of the water stops with no problem.

In fact, Rick and I have run 1,103 races!

When we announced that we were running in our last Boston Marathon, to our surprise they had a life-size statue built of Rick and me. It was unveiled one week before the race in Hakington, Massachusetts, just before the race started. The statue was only 200-300 yards from the starting line. Rick got to see it. It was amazing!

After decades of "flying" with Rick, we had created a foundation. People now run with the handicapped in the marathon for our foundation, every year. This year we had 32 runners. We all got together in Boston at the expo for three days. Rick and I got there three days before the marathon, and we sat on the cement floor. From this position we sold books and DVDs. People also talked to us and took photos. It was always an unbelievable week and sometimes we didn't even have a chance to go to the bathroom or eat, because it was wall-to-wall people. We always speak there, too. On Sunday, we met our foundation runners, many for the first time. We had a big pasta dinner and, on the morning of the marathon, we rented our own bus and met outside of the Sheraton Hotel at 5 o'clock in the morning. Then, we got a police escort to Boston.

The 2013 bombing was terrible.

The race started on a beautiful morning. All of the buses drove by our statue. It was the first time for many of our Hoyt Foundation runners to see it. It was beautiful. Some of them took group pictures. At the starting line, Channel 4 was ready. They always covered us live, at 8 o'clock in the morning, before the marathon started. So, Rick and I got going. We had a really good run, an hour ahead of last year's race. Then, when we got to the 23 mile mark, I noticed more police officers. When I stopped to ask an officer why, he said there had been two bombs detonated at the finish line.

It was heartbreaking.

We left the marathon only to discover that many of our runners were in the bleachers across the street from the finish line. Fortunately, none of our people or runners had been injured. But we still needed to get to reach the end of the race. When we passed the 25 mile marker, the police stopped us again. They told us that the marathon was over. We couldn't go any further. At the time we had 10 people from our foundation running with us. Rick was stuck in his running chair, because his everyday chair was in a VIP tent. (It had to stay there for three days because it was in the crime zone). Because Rick's running chair was so large, there was no way to transport him back to the Sheraton, since our van was inaccessible. Suddenly a man stepped out of the crowd and said, "Dick, I can get you as close to the Sheraton as possible." Our people took Rick's chair as I carried him over to the man's car.

We drove for an hour and a half because all of the streets were blocked off. When we got close to the Sheraton, the police stopped us, again, claiming we couldn't go any farther. The driver said, "Look, I've got Dick and Rick Hoyt here, and Rick doesn't have his wheelchair. We've got to get him to the front door of the Sheraton, now!" They saw us. They knew who we were, so they waved us through....

We were sad about the tragedy but grateful that everyone we knew escaped injury. We stayed there until all of our runners came in. It was a painful day.

Needless to say, the person who inspires me and gives me the motivation for Team Hoyt is my son, Rick. He is unbelievable. He is not a quitter. He never gives up! He is a fighter and has courage enough for anything. The life that he's lived is just unbelievable! To think about all of the running that was done; to think about him going to school and leaving his family. It took two hours to get into Boston. Think about someone who can't talk and uses his arms and legs, alone in the city of Boston going to BU. He hardly knew or personally met any of his personal care attendants. But, he went to Boston without any family members to help him.

It took Rick nine years to graduate from Boston University. But he did it.

It is unbelievable what has happened since he asked me to run in that first race. We never thought we would be doing marathons, triathlons . . . running across the United States and affecting people everywhere.

Since Rick was born, we tried to take him out in public. People were uncomfortable looking at him. They didn't want to talk to him or interact with him in schools. Especially, they didn't want him running. And look what's happened! Now we are invited all over the world. The first triathlon we ran was in Columbia. When we finished that, all the people had their front doors open and were playing "Chariots of Fire." They had a big parade of cars lined up behind us. We went across the finish line and they made us come back, turn around and cross it again.

In 1994–1995, we were invited to compete in Japan. In this country, I was told that they closet people with disabilities or challenges. They keep them inside. When we were over there, two of the biggest TV stations from Japan filmed documentaries about us. Now the handicapped can be seen outside there. In Germany we were treated like royalty. We went to El Salvador in 1995 when they were at war, to visit hospitals and schools in this impoverished country, and we spoke to them. The first night that we got there, we went out training on top of a hill. Suddenly, all these tanks and soldiers came at us. Fortunately for us, they were the good guys.

In El Salvador, they usually had 20 people to watch their triathlon. But when we were there, thousands of people showed up. They didn't believe that Rick and I were there doing what we were doing; they just saw that we were from the United States and thought that we were making movies. They had to call in the military to control the crowds. At the conclusion of this race, Rick and I never got to cross the finish line, because all these mothers and families wanted to shake our hands. They wanted us to hold and kiss their babies.

When we were out running, they had people with machine guns covering us. When we were out on the bikes, they had people in pickup trucks to protect us.

It has been unbelievable. We even got a call from China. They invited Rick and me to their China walk. There were people in despair in this country, even two ladies considering suicide. Now, after reading our story, they are out running triathlons. The list of benefits seems endless. There are drug addicts and alcoholics who have come clean because of our story.

All of this good has come into the world, all of these incredible events have been lived, because of one person.

My hero. My son, Rick!

EPILOGUE
The Quest for Kindness

The Past

On the last night of my career as a police officer in Las Vegas, I discovered fear as I have never known it. I lay crumpled on the pavement next to my patrol car as passersby snapped cell phone photos and videos of me. Wracked by a stroke, unable to speak or move, I was fully conscious and aware of everything around me, but trapped in an unresponsive body. I had lost my fear of death years before when I survived a firefight that by all rights I should not have. But on this night, I not only accepted the thought of death but prayed for it. The fear of the stroke taking away my capacity to move, to communicate, to make love, to touch another human being, was all consuming. I vividly recall the sweat dripping down my face as visions of my future bolted through my mind.

The call had gone out by my partner, a young patrol officer who was riding with me for the very first time. "Officer down, request paramedics." I was his lLieutenant, the watch commander on this fateful night, and his frantic radio report brought cops from throughout the city. "Officer down" . . . the worst words that can ever be broadcast in the police community. Within minutes that seemed to be hours my officers surrounded me in a protective circle and if I had been able to, I would have smiled as I heard one cop say to a camera-wielding tourist, "If you don't get that camera out of his face, I'm going to take it off you and stick it up your ass."

That was my last memory as an on-duty police officer, as the stroke ended my 34 years of proudly wearing a badge. The pain in my head seared through me as paramedics arrived and rushed me to the emergency room. I stared helplessly up at the Vegas neon and concerned faces of my officers and paramedics as they lifted me and shoved the gurney into the ambulance. I wanted to thank them, I wanted to embrace them, but couldn't. Tears of frustration and terror slipped down my face.

The Present

I am writing this as I travel on a flight back to my home in Las Vegas. I survived the stroke and subsequent heart surgery as well as the second stroke that struck me a few months later. I know I am incredibly fortunate that, apart from some memory loss, I can fully function again. But that night brought me something other than fear, pain and loss. It gave me an incredible gift . . . the gift of clarity. All of us have "WHY'S" that live within us. Why was I born into the family that I was? Why was I given this burden? Why did my life go into this direction? Each of us has asked these questions internally during moments of pain or challenge and sometimes even joy. The answers are elusive and rarely if ever come. That is the gift that I was given on that sweltering August night on the pavement, reeking of asphalt, stubbed-out cigarettes and the worn leather of a million shoes. I now know my mission.

The Quest

The life of a cop is a life poised against a backdrop of the entire spectrum of humanity and that, more frequently than not, is not a pretty picture. Each day can bring another assault on the senses that define us as human beings. Being a constant spectator to what people are capable of doing to each other can erode your soul and leave you feeling hollow inside. A shell of armor begins to build around your heart to protect you from the poison that long exposure to cruelty, greed, violence, and selfishness can infect you with. If this sounds slightly like a personal confession, then I will defer to your judgment, but to tell you the truth, I wouldn't have changed the life that I chose, for to serve others is the greatest honor that life can offer. Being a cop not only shows you the ugly side of life but also exposes you to others that share a sense of "mission," the mission to do your best to change this world in great or small ways and leave it just a little better than how you found it.

I saw thousands examples of men and women who believed that they can make a difference, not only in the ranks of law enforcement, but in everyday folks who I saw show kindness in so many ways I could never count. There was the woman I met while patrolling the roughest streets in Vegas, who nightly brought sandwiches to homeless people who were camped out beneath crude structures in the desert. The man who chose to mentor parentless children housed at the juvenile facility, or the organization that took on the task of building a monument to honor fallen police officers. Quite literally thousands of men and women who, though the pages of history may not remember, the countless people whose lives they touched will. They are the heroes and it is their stories that must be told.

We exist in a world where stories of faith and hope, kindness and compassion, integrity and honor are shunted aside by headlines exploding with misery, sadness, cruelty and greed. It has become difficult for many people to believe in anything or anyone as this epidemic of disillusionment spreads among us. The cure for this epidemic lies within each of us, individually and as a people. It is the greatest power on earth when harnessed for the greater good. It is the power of belief. Belief is the cornerstone of civilization; and when it is nurtured and enriched by parents who provide love, by friends who provide support and by people who live the values of kindness, compassion, integrity and honor, it flowers within us and creates a better world.

For thirty-four years my mission as a law enforcement officer was to protect and serve the people of my community. While that mission has ended for me, the gift of clarity, which came to me through loss and grief has shown me my new "mission" and I accept it with honor and respect. Not only shall I personally live the principles that I hold so dear, but I will celebrate the legacies of the countless men and women who are touching the lives of others in great and small ways by honoring them and their accomplishments in word and deed. By sharing the stories of these amazing people, I believe that others will be inspired to follow in their footsteps and thus lead more fulfilling lives themselves.

I thank you for reading this book and sincerely hope that you found yourself not only enjoying the stories but thinking about how you might be able to reach out to someone and make a difference. I know that you can, because I believe.

- I believe that each of us has the ability to change the world.
- I believe that each smile that we create on the face of another person touches that person's life.
- I believe that when we give of ourselves, we give TO ourselves.
- I believe that most people wish to be better than they are and that is and of itself a defining characteristic of humanity.
- I believe that friendship is the purist form of love.
- I believe that personal honor is born of the wisdom and morality of those who have experienced life and its many joys and disappointments and passed on those lessons to those they love.
- I believe that charity lives on in all of us but will only be released to others when we have accepted our own human frailties and weaknesses.
- I believe that there can be no greater honor than to be given the trust of another, and no greater dishonor than to betray it.
- I believe that how you are remembered by those whose lives you have touched will determine your true success and the legacy that you leave behind.
- I believe that our legacy is not about what we do tomorrow, it is about what we do today.

THE END